SCRAPS,
WILT
+
WEEDS

SCRAPS, WILT + WEEDS

Turning Wasted Food into Plenty

MADS REFSLUND

& TAMA MATSUOKA WONG

GRAND CENTRAL
Life&Style
NEW YORK · BOSTON

Grand Central Life & Style
Hachette Book Group
1290 Avenue of the Americas, New York, NY 10104
grandcentrallifeandstyle.com
twitter.com/grandcentralpub

First Edition: March 2017

Grand Central Life & Style is an imprint of Grand Central Publishing.
The Grand Central Life & Style name and logo are trademarks of
Hachette Book Group, Inc.

The publisher is not responsible for websites (or their content)
that are not owned by the publisher.

The Hachette Speakers Bureau provides a wide range
of authors for speaking events. To find out more, go to
www.hachettespeakersbureau.com or call (866) 376-6591.

Library of Congress Cataloging-in-Publication Data has
been applied for.

ISBNs: 978-1-4555-3615-3 (hardcover), 978-1-4555-3617-7 (ebook)

Printed in the United States of America

Q-MA

10 9 8 7 6 5 4 3 2 1

TO
THE EARTH
AND ALL HER PARTS—
LAND
AIR
WATER
LIFE
AND DECAY

INTRO:

TURNING GARBAGE
INTO GOLD xi

1
RIPE
FOR
REVOLUTION
1

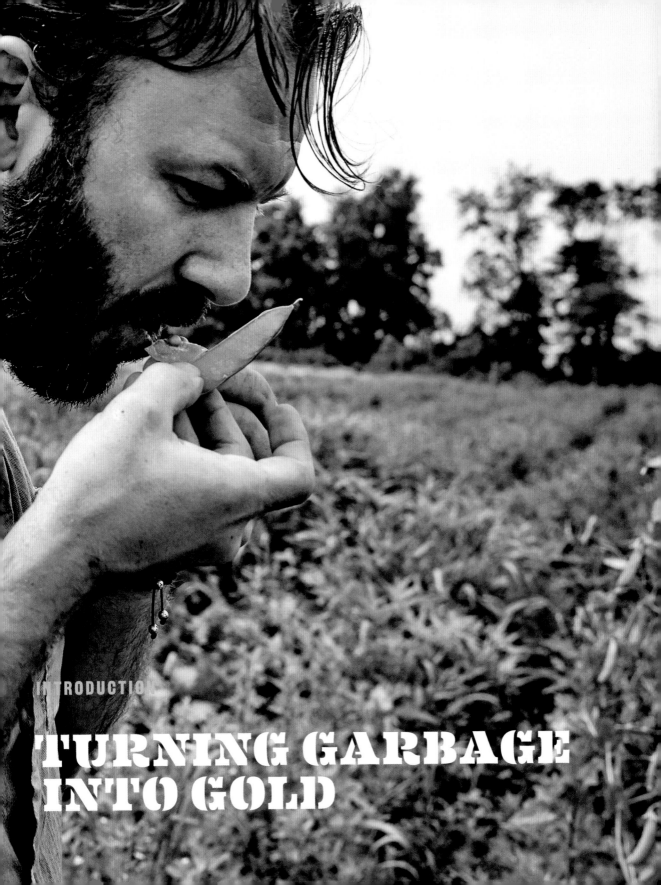

TURNING GARBAGE INTO GOLD

I COME FROM DENMARK; IT IS A GOOD COUNTRY, ALTHOUGH FOR MUCH OF THE YEAR IT IS DARK AND COLD.

I HAVE HEARD THAT the United Nations rated Danes number one in "happiness," but in terms of money, the Danish economy doesn't come even close to the top ten. How can people feel happy through such bleak winters? I think Danes do worry a lot, but they have a long tradition of resilience, of making plenty out of nothing, with little more than our own labor and the human spirit of creativity.

We celebrate the beauty of food from nature, like so many other cultures of the world. We can't grow food for many months of the year, so we are forced to rely on crafting methods to survive well, through the dark times: fermentation, brining, drying, curing. It is normal to eat all parts and scraps, wasting little. So maybe it's more about a way of life that makes people feel rich, turning garbage into gold.

But of course we now live in a globalized world with its lure of luxurious and exotic ingredients: spices like harissa and saffron; truffles; tropical fruits—all from faraway places with less harsh climates than ours. Everyone always wants to get their hands on these things, but not me.

When I was at culinary school in Copenhagen, the day would begin with a cart full of ingredients to cook from. I would wait for the other chefs to pick first. I waited to see what they would grab, because I wanted to take the things left at the bottom—forsaken because they were ugly or took too long to cook. I wanted to make them delicious, and to honor them: beautiful gifts from nature. Others would choose the prime rib or langoustine. I would choose the root vegetables.

Because after all what is good food and what is trash? "Trash" and "scraps" are ideas that people create when they decide what is in and what is out. "Civilized cultures" decide what is luxury and what is rubbish. Who made these rules?

Instead I am inspired by nature's rules. In nature, there is no ugly, no trash, just cycles of change. Good food must embrace nature. A beautiful ingredient is unique, each plant a little bit different, not perfect as if it were produced in a factory. I found that I wanted to work with honest ingredients, with what I see and touch in front of me. Unlike overprocessed food, meals with ingredients that are closer to nature are alive with flavor notes and nuances.

I came to America from Copenhagen less than five years ago. I fell in love with the city and a girl and decided to move here, to New York City. New York is different from Copenhagen. New York is a city packed with 20 million people instead of 2 million: exciting and diverse people and food from all over the world. Even when I decided that I would get only local products, I found the markets were full of a vegetable and fruit bounty I only dreamed of in Denmark.

But even with all these great choices, I find it funny that many Americans across the country still pretty much eat the same kinds of foods, from four plants: rice, wheat, corn, and soybeans.

Previous spread:
Eating peas in the field with Farmer Mark.

Left:
Charred root vegetables.

And many people eat their meals in a kind of automated way, the same twenty-five produce items over and over, like living in a self-imposed Danish winter. I wanted to try new things, like the native pawpaw fruit or the spicebush berry. Why do the people living here not care about their own native fruits or the trees around them? Why do people not eat salmon with the skin on or have a hunk of cauliflower at the center of the plate? Why does a dessert have to be a cake with lots of artificial icing instead of using the natural sweetness of beets or wheatgrass? I didn't want to just play it safe and make a stereotypical version of burgers and fries, pizza, or some kind of heavy sauce around a pork chop. I wanted juicy, refreshing, and light meals with great flavor.

And there is a lot of great flavor in the food that people threw out: in garbage bags with uneaten food piled up on the sidewalks, in markets, kitchens, dumpsters, trash bins, and even on docks and farms. I didn't get turned off by the grittiness, the garbage. I saw an opportunity. I started getting really excited about bringing the philosophies that began for me in Denmark to my new home in America. I also liked the downtown casual lifestyle. Some of the best meals I've eaten are simple and clean, layered with flavor and conversation. It's the spirit of what we call *hygge*: "coziness," meaning good living.

When I was young, in Denmark, my parents took time off from work for a few years, and we lived on an island. It was kind of a farm. They had a vision and created a home-stay program, sponsored by the Danish government. Their idea was to create an oasis to help people with troubles get better through nature, food, and a place to stay. There is a kind of poetry about that kind of life, so close to the outdoors. I still see it today in the shapes and textures of vegetables, fruit, fish, and meat as they are made, whole in the outdoors, not decapitated and made pretty for consumers.

I seek nature in food, by cooking and serving it on the plate. I always start by wanting to see what the produce is like whole, the way it was living in nature. Yes, with dirt and guts and tough parts. Each of these parts is important and has a role in the life of that species and is beautiful in its own way. Using all the parts is a way of respecting the plant, the fish, the animal, and its life. Of course, you have to set aside the parts that have poisons, such as apple seeds, but there are ways to tenderize the tough, to puree the wilted, and make the most of the basic character of a native plant or animal. Look at their strengths, not their weaknesses. They may still have a beautiful color, even if misshapen. Their shriveled structure may mean they are already on their way to becoming dried.

For me, cooking has got to start with this view.

I am also curious about the different stages of food: when it was young, flowered, bore fruit and progeny, and later becomes old and shriveled. People have found the key to making magic out of aged goods such as cheese, dry aged meat, and wine for centuries. I just want to unlock the flavor from other "aged" goods like stale bread, wrinkly root vegetables, wilted leafy greens, sour milk, overripe fruits, flat beer.

As a chef who sources food from purveyors, I also see a lot of potential in using waste products from the preparation and processing of food: cheese rinds, coffee grounds, juice pulp, the bran of grains like wheat and rice. These are all part of the whole; these parts have simply been transformed and reshaped.

When I first started living in New York City, I had this idea that I would be able to go out to nature every day or several times a week, like I did in Copenhagen. I asked people: *Where is the wild?* I learned that the wild is either a park owned by the government or private property. You can't just go around picking things in nature as you can in Denmark, where there is a "right to roam" (as long as it is not for commercial purposes and you respect nature). And it takes a lot longer to get out of the city, so I could only go out on the weekends to re-inspire myself.

When I finally got out of the city to a farm or forest, I saw food all around me that nobody seemed to notice. The same plants I recognized from my days at NOMA and in Copenhagen, like the bolted vegetable flowers, the chickweed, and the Norway spruce tree. People here don't even think of these plants as food, even though their ancestors probably enjoyed many of them. This can be the best kind of food—straight from nature—and it belongs in every dish.

But instead, what usually ends up in the dish, what many think of as a "meal," is why there is so much waste. A classic protein-heavy hunk of meat or fillet of fish means a lot of the animal is wasted, and raising livestock and over-fishing puts stress on our natural resources. I like to put the vegetable at the center of the plate, or use meat or fish as the flavoring, or put the vegetable in the dessert. It's lighter and more refreshing.

And of course, great food must have its identity, from a time and place, not only where we are now but also where we come from. My cooking reflects much of my homeland: natural shapes and colors, hardy vegetables and berries, fish and herbs, pickles and dairy. But I have no dishes here with reindeer meat or sea buckthorn. Instead, I have come to love the banana, corn on the cob, watermelon, pumpkin.

I don't pretend that I, or anyone, invented the idea of cooking from scraps. This is the way people have lived frugally—to survive—from the beginning of humanity, bound with the rhythms of the seasons. So the methods and recipes in this book have their roots in the memories of how people have always prepared and enjoyed food—as the center of life—by preserving, fermenting, drying, and grilling, and making use of what was around them.

So it is with humbleness that I am inspired by the generations and cultures that came before. I hope, through this book, to inspire in you the excitement of using time-honored ways and, at the same time, to be practical and to start cooking with the scraps, wilt, and weeds that you are used to throwing out, no matter where you are living and whatever your budget.

When you decide to look at things through a low-waste cooking lens, you start to look at recipes differently. A standard recipe usually tells readers that they must start with only the most perfect produce: "Make sure that it has no blemishes, no bruises, is evenly shaped, with no signs of yellow or insect holes." I won't be saying any of that here.

It's okay for a fruit or vegetable to have a blemish, be misshapen, to show a little bruise or two. Insect holes are fine.

Have a little fun.

FROM MAKING FUN TO MAKING CUISINE:
TRASH COOKING

I THINK IT WAS MY FORMER ROOMMATE René Redzepi who first used the words *trash cooking* at NOMA restaurant in Denmark. He said, speaking of the long Danish winter:

One of the constant themes of winter, year in and year out, is waste. Because we have so little to work with, what we throw in the bin causes us real pain. We've made fun of it so many times, "cooking out of the trash bin," but it was always meant to be a joke, even though for ethical reasons I love the idea of wasting nothing. But for it to actually become a guide to deliciousness, you have to restrain yourself, for it can take you down some unconventional paths...

All the guys in the test kitchen perked up when I said, "Trash cooking, people. I'm not saying this as a joke anymore—why don't we let it steer us?" A project where we build dishes out of the refuse that would normally find its way to the dumpster: vegetable peelings, meat trimmings, things like that...

And the chefs liked this idea, because it challenged cultural ideologies and replaced them with the concept that "all ingredients have the same worth." It felt good to break down the rules about what is luxury and what is rubbish.

When I cook, I'm, of course, not taking things out of the garbage. But it's important to pause, even for just a moment, before making the decision to throw food away. Cooking with scraps must start with knowing how things grow and live as a whole, in nature, even if sometimes they are "imperfect" or "ugly," or have become wilted and wrinkled.

Then try to see it a different way. Instead of slimy fish skin, see crispy umami. Instead of mushy fruit, see succulent fermented glaze.

I'm not settling for less by using wasted things. Of course, as many chefs in restaurants do, I want to be—I must be—more economical. But when I use what everyone else thinks is scrap or trash, I want to crack the code so that the taste is enriching, enticing, and deep: layers of flavors, not just salt and sugar.

HOW TO USE THIS BOOK

THE FIRST PART, and the bulk of this book, is organized by ingredient—whether vegetable, fruit, fish, meat, grain, or dairy—so that you can easily find a particular item you would usually throw away. We start each ingredient's section by explaining factual information about the "edible anatomy" of the produce, what parts are normally wasted, along with cultural anecdotes, and more.

The photos and Mads's dishes remain authentic to his style, although simplified for home cooking. I have supplemented these with some additional cultural and historical methods of preparation in sections called "Other Ways to Enjoy…" to give you a range of choices, along with a few additional recipes. My recipes are marked with my initials, and are a little more informal.

I include a chapter with some strategies for pragmatically making use of leftovers by mastering easy yet versatile dishes and for stocking about a dozen basic ingredients in the home kitchen.

And finally, to go beyond your own pantry and into (and beyond!) your backyard: The last section is about using foraged or found plants as delicious ingredients that are usually ignored and certainly wasted.

Jan Wong

1

RIPE FOR REVOLUTION

What We Throw Away

Food waste is a big deal. In the United States alone, 40 percent of food goes uneaten, amounting to about $162 billion a year. Globally, 33 percent of food is unused: $750 billion worth of food that is produced is lost or wasted every year. Food waste is now the largest component of what goes into landfills and incinerators.

The waste of food occurs at almost every juncture in the supply chain: from blemished crops that lie unharvested in the fields, to further culling of produce and other food parts bruised or deemed unfit during processing, to the dead or dying seafood that is thrown back into the ocean. Supermarkets and grocery stores threw out 43 billion pounds of food in 2010. But above all, as Dana Gunders informs us, "Consumers are responsible for more wasted food than farmers, grocery stores, or any other part of the food supply chain… The lettuce that went bad, the leftovers you never got around to eating, and that scary science experiment in the back of the refrigerator." Americans are throwing away an average of $120 each month per household of four in the form of uneaten food.

Although the data is not complete, of the 133 billion pounds of food loss in the United States in 2010 at the retail and consumer levels, topping the list by food group are: 25.4 billion pounds of dairy and 25.2 billion pounds of vegetables (19 percent each), and 18.5 billion pounds of grain and 18.4 billion pounds of fruit (14 percent each).

Ultimately, wasting food is a decision. Each person, every household, decides what to buy and what they like to eat more of, as well as the parts to avoid because they are too ugly, too tough. Food waste is partly a value judgment about what is desirable and what is not. In the words of William Rathje and Cullen Murphy in *Rubbish!: The Archeology of Garbage*: "What people have owned—and thrown away—can speak more eloquently, informatively, and truthfully about the lives they lead than they themselves ever may."

This chapter relies heavily on the expertise, research, and numerous conversations with Dana Gunders, staff scientist for the Natural Resources Defense Council and author of *Waste Free Kitchen Handbook*, as well as an interview with Jonathan Bloom, author of *American Wasteland*. See the Works Consulted section on page 276 for more information.

Why Is So Much Food Wasted?

MYTH:
Cosmetically perfect produce is superior produce.

Many fruits and vegetables are passed over because they are just not "perfect." They have a bend in the root or an indentation. These blemished specimens never make it to the markets, and as much as 30 percent of produce never makes it past the farms. Some companies, such as Bon Appétit and Imperfect Produce, have begun to buy ugly produce, recognizing that these items are just as tasty as "perfect" produce, even though they have been rejected by retailers.

MYTH:
Bigger is better.

Portion sizes, in restaurants as well as at home, have increased exponentially, and are now 2 to 8 times larger than recommended serving sizes. Soda cups started in 1955 at 7 ounces; more recently, McDonald's offered the Supersize (the name has changed since) soda at 42 ounces and 7-Eleven has the Double Big Gulp at 64 ounces and the Team Gulp at 128 ounces (that's 1 gallon, 1,490 calories). The average adult stomach holds only 30 ounces.

Refrigerators are getting bigger: Over time, refrigerators have become available in larger and larger sizes. Although the refrigerator is a great invention, prolonging the life of food by keeping it chilled and ready to use, it has also enabled people to think less about preserving food. The larger the fridge, the more things become pushed to the back to decay. If not in plain sight, the food is forgotten.

MYTH:
Expiration
dates on a carton
mean that the food
has gone bad.

Many foods that are sold in supermarkets and other retail establishments have a stamped expiration date. A lot of food that has gone past the stamped date on a package doesn't look bad, and there is confusion about whether that date means the food is no longer fit to eat. The dates are not actual spoilage dates, but rather recommendations by the manufacturer for when the food is at peak quality. Other labels include language such as "Sell by," "Best before," and "Enjoy by," which adds to the confusion. Although no study has yet been conducted in the United States, a study in the United Kingdom estimates 20 percent of avoidable household food waste is due to confusion over expiration dates. What these phrases all have in common, though, is this: They are not an indicator of when food becomes unsafe to eat, but rather what manufacturers provide retailers to assist in rotating stock and inventory. They are based on certain value judgments that some-one is making about when food looks good, as well as assumptions about what the food is to be used for.

Although much of the food purchased by consumers has been trans-ported long distances and stored somewhere along the way, consumers still buy food based on the illusion of "freshness," meaning large sized, unblemished, shiny, and brightly colored.

SO WHEN *IS* FOOD NO LONGER GOOD, I.E., NOT SAFE TO EAT?

WHEN PEOPLE STARTED buying their food and growing less and less of it, they lost confidence in their ability to tell, through smell and taste, if a food was spoiled. If food smells bad or has become moldy, even before the stamped date, throw it out. Most commonly, shellfish, but also prepackaged sandwiches, eggs, infant formula, shucked oysters, and milk are potentially hazardous when spoiled and must be refrigerated to remain safe. The key is to keep them in optimal storage conditions, which is 40°F and below. Leaving food unchilled, out on the counter, may render it unsafe, even prior to its expiration date. Dana Gunders's *Waste Free Kitchen Handbook* contains a useful directory with spoilage information for common food products.

Wilted and Old Food: Preserving It

We are obsessed with the pursuit of freshness. There is something impressively alive about anything that is just picked or just caught. The texture is springy. The aroma fills the senses. The enemy is time, and as it passes, the food reaches the point when it is wilted and old and then, finally, becomes moldy and rotten, when it must almost certainly be thrown away.

But for centuries humanity has fought this passage of time and the creep of rottenness. People survived with marvelous inventions for keeping and preserving food, antidotes to wasting food.

Unlike a date on a carton, the process of aging is waiting for time to pass. Food isn't perfect one day, and then suddenly when the stamped date arrives, "oh no," it is instantly old and bad. Dairy, changing from milk to butter to yogurt to cheese, is a great example of aging as a process.

Fermentation, drying, canning, and pickling are ways to avoid food waste, to make use of abundant food, and to distill distinct flavors. These basic and time-honored methods span the globe and are found across cultures. Today they are being reinvented as a basis for creating nutritious and flavor-rich food. They also are ways of respecting and reducing food waste.

It is an admirable craft and skill to know how to ferment, to brine, to preserve food from the season. And what's more, the flavor is more intense. We should know these things at all stages of their life and not disregard their process of aging. Sometimes we may have to wait, but waiting and the anticipation makes the appreciation even better when the food is ready, like a good wine or cheese. Finding and trying new ingredients in new ways reveals that cured pumpkin is amazing, and that pickled flower petals and buds are fantastic.

The processes are very natural and depend on the forces of nature for preservation:

HEATING: Food that has been cooked keeps better than raw food does. If you have a piece of raw meat or fish but not a lot of time to make an elaborate meal, cooking it means you have more time before you must eat it. Canning food is an extension of the heating process, preserving food at high temperatures in a glass container, which is then sealed and the air removed to prevent spoilage. Canning will extend the life of produce for a year or more.

FREEZING: Freezing can kill parasites as well as extend the life of food for some time. Wrap the food tightly in plastic wrap and then foil in order to keep quality high. Buying something already frozen generally means that the nutrient value may not be compromised, due to more advanced flash freezing technology. When buying frozen food, buy items that have been manipulated (chopped, pureed, etc.) as little as possible before freezing.

DRYING: Drying food is another ancient method of preserving food. Drying inhibits the growth of bacteria and mold. Today there are drying screens, dehydrators, and low-set ovens. Drying can intensify the flavors of ingredients.

FERMENTATION: Fermentation is the "flavorful space between fresh and rotten," according to Sandor Katz, fermentation teacher and author of *The Art of Fermentation*. Sandor recommends that fermentation enthusiasts not become paralyzed by having to follow exact measurements. Fermentation adds layers of flavor; some of the most flavorful, exciting food and beverages in fact rely on fermentation: wine, beer, cheese, yogurt, pickles, vinegar, miso. In addition, fermented food is good for the health. Studies are finding that feeding the bacteria in the gut is essential to human health. The Human Microbiome Project has begun cataloguing these "good" bacteria and their importance in digestion, immune system functionality, obesity, and brain function. Foods with probiotics, i.e., fermented food, help to keep the gut healthy.

BRINING WITH SALT: Brining is a traditional and natural way to preserve foods. It activates the natural bacteria in fresh vegetables and converts them to lactic acid plus CO_2 (which forms bubbles). Bonus: This fermentation process naturally produces probiotics, which can aid digestion. See page 120.

PICKLING WITH VINEGAR: See page 45.

SUGAR PRESERVING: Jams and jellies use heat and sugar to preserve produce.

ALCOHOL: Is a natural preservative for fruits and aromatics. See page 119.

From the beginning of history, our ability to survive depended on wasting little. The wisdom of cultures ingeniously preserved what bounty nature offered. Food was a product of nature: rough, unrefined, and not shrink-wrapped. In the everyday rush of modern urbanized living, we have lost the sense of connection with tradition and nature. The rest of this book focuses on getting it back.

Opposite: Picking fallen fruit at Grow a Row Farm.

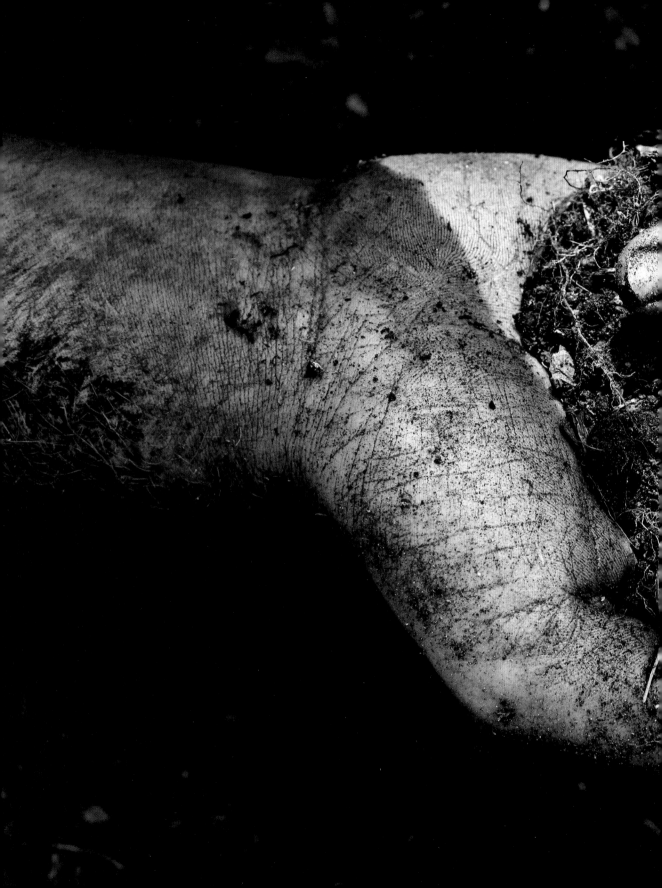

COMPOST

THROWING FOOD SCRAPS into the garbage can or down the sink's garbage disposal eventually just adds more bulk to municipal waste. Home composting is preferable to sending things to a landfill. Less than 5 percent of food waste is composted.

All vegetable and fruit produce, baked goods, pasta, grains, rice, coffee grounds, and eggshells can be composted.

The following items are not advisable to compost because they attract animals, including rats, and sometimes maggots: meat or meat products, fish, dairy, and grease or oils (these also do not biodegrade well into the soil).

2

VEGETABLES

To me, a vegetable is most beautiful
in its original state: whole, with the
soil still clinging to its roots.

BEFORE I CAN DECIDE how to eat a plant, I need to see each of its parts—the top, the skin, and, of course, the core (the body, the heart of the plant)—and hold them in my hands.

I devote a lot of time to thinking about vegetables. And why not? Their character—shapes, colors, tastes, textures—vary greatly. Some of my favorite vegetables are the ones I call *meaty:* potatoes, cauliflower, cabbage, and broccoli. They have enough heft to show off at the center of the plate. I also love juicy and crunchy vegetables, such as celery, fennel, or purslane, especially when raw and shaved thin.

Root vegetables hold a special place in my heart because they are literally pulled from the earth. While Americans don't typically get excited about them, in Denmark potatoes, carrots, beets, and all the others are staples over the long winter, and we are still discovering ways to unlock their flavors.

It's important to know that if you have been boiling root vegetables, you have not been doing them any favors. Boiling overcooks them on the outside and undercooks them on the inside. Instead, root vegetables are much better roasted with the skins on. Plus, there is no waste.

My favorite way to cook vegetables is to grill them over fire. Grilling releases the flavor and gives a little bit of smoky char to the vegetable. In the summertime, when people are enjoying a good barbecue with meat, it is so easy to add vegetables. Even in the winter, if you don't have a fire, dry searing in a cast iron skillet, using a grill pan, or charring slightly over the flame on a gas stove will brown the outside and seal in the flavor of even the most humble looking vegetable. And it's simple to vary the flavors by using lots of herbs, lemon, salt, and pepper.

Most people don't see the entire vegetable, and they use just one or two parts of the plant in a meal. In this chapter, we'll look at each vegetable as a whole, and celebrate all its parts—particularly those that are commonly discarded. Because when you start using the whole vegetable, you start to see that it just doesn't make common sense to throw away, for example, the entire bulk of the pea plant to eat only the peas.

My favorite
way to cook
vegetables is
to grill them
over fire.

BEETS

I LOVE THE SURREAL COLOR OF BEETS. It is hard to imagine that their gorgeous shade—more vibrant than most flowers—develops beneath the ground. Beets' slightly earthy, smoky, and sweet flavor goes well with fruits like cherries and blueberries.

I never peel beets. If there is dirt on them, I just scrub it off. And the parts most commonly discarded—the above-ground tops and stems—are wonderful to eat. Although they keep well in the refrigerator, over time beets become wrinkled and soft and then later wrinkled and dry. But as long as they are not covered in mold, or slimy and rotten, they are fine to eat.

BEET TOP & STEM SALSA

I purposely don't call tops of beets the *beet greens* because the stems are beautifully red. Make sure you include the stems.

1 cup finely chopped beet tops
1 cup finely chopped beet stems
¼ cup blueberries, wrinkled is fine
¼ cup apple cider vinegar

In a medium bowl, toss to combine the ingredients. Do not blend.

TESTER'S NOTE:
The stems were not at all stringy, but crunchy like celery. I stuffed this inside an avocado sandwich instead of lettuce.

MAKES 2 CUPS / TIME: 15 MIN

BEET JUICE VINAIGRETTE

This dressing serves as a base flavor in Marinated Beet Tops & Stems (at right) and Dried Beets (page 25).

1 cup beet juice, from a home juicer or local juice or smoothie shop
2 tablespoons red wine vinegar
1 tablespoon lemon juice
2 tablespoons extra virgin olive oil
½ teaspoon kosher salt

In a small pot over low heat, simmer the beet juice for 45 minutes, until reduced by half. In a small bowl, whisk together the reduced beet juice, red wine vinegar, lemon juice, olive oil, and salt.

MAKES ABOUT ⅔ CUP; SERVES 4 / TIME: 1 HR

MARINATED BEET TOPS & STEMS

4 beet tops and stems, finely chopped
¼ cup Beet Juice Vinaigrette (at left)

Mix the chopped stems with the vinaigrette and let marinate for at least 15 minutes before serving.

SERVES 4 / TIME: 20 MIN

Opposite: Hands and beet greens by Mark Canwright of Comeback Farm.

Beet
Picnic

Wrap vegetable scraps in a
Beet Pulp Crepe (page 27),
dressed with Carrot Top Pesto
(page 51), and serve with
Fire-Roasted Beets (page 25),
Dried Beets (page 25), and
Kale Chips (page 73). Enjoy
this picnic.

FIRE-ROASTED BEETS

The best way to cook beets is to slow roast, not boil them, to bring out the earthy smokiness and intensify the sweetness. Roast them over a bonfire and pass them around with lemon wedges and salt. So simple and good. If you don't have a fire, use an oven or grill.

4 to 6 medium to large red beets, scrubbed but not peeled (save the tops and stems for **Beet Top & Stem Salsa, page 20**)
1 lemon, halved
Salt, to taste

Wrap the beets in foil. If I have access to a fire pit, I put the wrapped beets right in the embers, to slow cook for about an hour. But since I don't know the temperature of the fire, I test for doneness by sticking a knife into the beets after 40 minutes; when it goes through cleanly, the beets are done.

The wrapped beets can also be roasted in a 400°F oven for 40 minutes, until a knife goes through them easily.

Unwrap the beets from the foil and let cool. Cut into wedges and season with a squeeze of lemon and salt.

SERVES 4 / TIME: 1 HR

DRIED BEETS

I sometimes call these Forgotten Beets, because they make the most of beets that have been left sitting in the bottom of the refrigerator drawer. Lucky for us forgetful cooks, rehydrating after drying them makes them chewy and sweet. Serve as part of the Beet Picnic (page 23) or with a beet granita (see Carrot Top Granita, page 50) and whipped yogurt for dessert.

8 to 12 whole red beets, ugly, misshapen, and wrinkled is great, scrubbed but not peeled and cut into 2-inch logs
3 tablespoons vegetable oil
2 tablespoons red wine vinegar
1 tablespoon kosher salt
⅔ cup **Beet Juice Vinaigrette** (page 20)
Special equipment: Dehydrator with temperature gage.

In a medium bowl, toss the beets with the oil, vinegar, and salt. Dehydrate at 150°F (or dry in the oven; see page 27) for 6 hours, until they are completely dry and shriveled.

Store immediately in an airtight container for up to 6 months. When ready to serve, reconstitute in the Beet Juice Vinaigrette for 1 hour.

SERVES 4 / ACTIVE TIME: 10 MIN / TOTAL TIME: 6 HRS or longer

BEET CHILI SAUCE

I toss this slightly spicy sauce with Beet Pulp Wide Pasta (page 31), then finish with shavings of salted fish or meat, and lemon juice to taste. You can also use this in place of other chili or hot sauces.

½ cup (1 stick) unsalted butter
4 cups beet juice, from a home juicer or local juice or smoothie shop
2 tablespoons Asian chili bean sauce

In a small pot, combine the butter, beet juice, and chili bean sauce and bring to a boil. Reduce the heat to medium-low and cook until the sauce is reduced by half, about 30 minutes.

MAKES 2 CUPS, 4 SERVINGS / TIME: 30 TO 40 MIN

BEET PULP CREPES

These crepes don't have a strong beet flavor, so they can easily be stuffed with whatever ingredients you choose without worrying about how those ingredients will go with beets. The color is beautiful and a great intro to using vegetable pulp in ordinary baked or flour recipes.

2 large eggs
1¼ cups milk
¾ cup all-purpose flour
¼ cup Beet Pulp Powder (right)
3 tablespoons unsalted butter, plus additional butter for the pan
¼ teaspoon salt

In a medium bowl, combine the eggs, milk, flour, beet powder, butter, and salt. Chill in the refrigerator for 30 minutes or up to 48 hours.

Heat an 8-inch nonstick pan over medium heat and melt a dab of butter in the pan to coat it. Pour about ¼ cup batter into the pan, swirling to spread it evenly. Cook for 30 seconds, then flip and cook on the other side for another 10 seconds, until lightly browned. Remove and let cool. Continue with the rest of the batter to make about 12 crepes, adding dabs of butter from time to time if the pan becomes too dry.

To serve, stack the crepes, and let each person choose their favorite filling to slather on one side of a crepe and then fold in half and then once again in quarters. They will store well for several days in plastic bags in the refrigerator.

MAKES 12 CREPES, 6 SERVINGS / ACTIVE TIME: 1 HR / INACTIVE TIME: 30 MIN

BEET PULP POWDER

I love how colorful this looks using beets. You can pulp and dry other vegetables as well.

2 cups beet pulp, leftover from home juicing or from a local juice bar

Use a dehydrator with a temperature gage or, alternatively, preheat the oven, to 150°F. Spread the beet pulp on a baking sheet. Dehydrate for 8 to 10 hours, or dry in the oven, until completely dry. Store in an airtight container without direct exposure to light for up to 6 months. When ready to use, grind to a fine powder in a spice or coffee grinder.

MAKES ¼ CUP / ACTIVE TIME: 10 MIN / TOTAL TIME: 8 TO 10 HRS

DEHYDRATING

If you do not have a dehydrator, you can use the oven, preheated to the lowest setting. Leave plenty of room for air circulation in order to dry thoroughly, using the oven's convection setting if available. If you live in an area with little to no humidity, you may be able to dehydrate using simply a pilot light in your oven; however, these instructions are designed to work for any area. It is also important to store your dried produce immediately in an airtight, sealed container; if you leave it open and it is very humid, they can start to rehydrate and begin to spoil.

WASTING VEGETABLE
PULP AND *WASTED*:
DAN
BARBER'S
POP-UP

LEFTOVER PULP from fruit and vegetable juice is a good way to add flavor, moistness, and nutrients to a variety of dishes, from veggie burgers, to muffins, to soups and stews. I was first inspired to use vegetable pulps by Dan Barber, chef and co-owner of Blue Hill and Blue Hill at Stone Barns. Dan is very much an educator and a superb speaker, whether at the Stone Barns Center for Food and Agriculture or traveling to learn about what people are doing around the world and telling their stories to influence food policies and practices.

It started over dinner at ACME where I used to cook, when I told Dan I was writing a book on cooking from waste. He was so enthusiastic and supportive that he closed down his Manhattan restaurant to run a three-week pop-up dinner series in 2015 called WastED, to educate people about food that is wasted. Dan invited guest chefs, challenging them to think about and cook creatively from food waste.

As a participant (and a diner) in this series, I was fascinated by the research that Dan was doing—finding uses for waste by-products generated by large scale food processing and smaller (but no less delicious) food waste, such as water from canned chickpeas, whipped into foam—a substitute for egg whites. I became a bit preoccupied with vegetable pulp after the dinner and got to know all the neighborhood juice bars, taking away their leftover pulp. You see in this book how I put it to use.

BEET PULP WIDE PASTA

The beet powder is nice formed into a wide and flat shaped pasta like a pappardelle. I serve them with Beet Chili Sauce (page 25) and Cured Tuna Bloodline (page 192). Cook the pasta in a large pot of salted boiling water for 90 seconds, or until just barely done, then toss with herbs such as mint or parsley or your favorite pesto sauce.

3 cups all-purpose flour
¼ cup Beet Pulp Powder (page 27)
1 teaspoon kosher salt
Semolina flour, for dusting
3 large eggs plus 3 egg yolks, beaten
1 tablespoon olive oil

In a medium bowl, combine the flour, beet powder, and salt.

On a lightly floured surface, make a well out of the flour mixture and pour the eggs and olive oil into the center. Gradually incorporate the sides of the well into the egg, working in more flour until the dough is moist but no longer wet. Knead the dough vigorously for 20 minutes, until firm but still moist. (Alternatively, you can knead the dough in a mixer with a dough hook for 5 to 10 minutes, following the mixer instructions.) Add flour if the dough is too sticky, or spritz with water if it is too dry or crumbly.

Wrap the dough in plastic and chill in the refrigerator for at least 30 minutes, or ideally overnight.

Dust two baking sheets liberally with semolina flour.

Cut the dough in quarters and press flat.

Roll each quarter (keeping the remaining quarters of dough wrapped) at least 3 times through a pasta rolling machine, starting at the thickest setting, and adjusting to progressively thinner settings, until ⅛ inch thick. (Note: On most pasta machines, either the last or second-to-last setting is best for pappardelle.)

Cut the pasta wide, into about 1-inch ribbons.

MAKES 1¼ POUNDS PASTA, 4 SERVINGS /
ACTIVE TIME: 35 MIN by hand/10 MIN by machine /
INACTIVE TIME: 30 MIN or overnight

Other Uses for Vegetable Pulp

VEGGIE PULP BURGERS

Add to the "burger" in place of beans or other filler.

JUICE PULP MUFFINS

Substitute the pulp for the shredded carrot in your favorite carrot muffin recipe.

SOUPS AND STEWS

Add a cup or more to thicken your vegetable or meat based soup or stew.

BROCCOLI

MOST OF US THINK OF BROCCOLI as the flowerhead, but that makes up a mere fraction of the overall plant. A member of the cabbage family, the broccoli plant boasts huge fleshy leaves that rarely make it to the market shelves but are perfectly edible. And its central leader trunk, or the *stem* in botanic terms, is often dismissed as tough. But in reality, it is actually meaty, mild, and crunchy—not unlike winter asparagus. In fact, the stalk or stem of vegetables is so prized in Chinese cooking, that there is a vegetable (called *wosun* or celtuce) that is grown specifically for the thick stem.

BROCCOLI STEMS WITH LARDO & FRESH CORIANDER SEEDS

½ cup (1 stick) unsalted butter

4 large broccoli stems, trimmed of their bases and woody skin (reserve those for Vegetable Scrap & Peel Stock, page 230)

2 tablespoons green coriander seeds, coriander flower bouquets, and stems (see page 263 in the Foraging chapter)

2 large heads Roasted Ugly Garlic (page 64)

3 ounces thinly sliced lardo (or prosciutto, torn into 2-inch pieces), chilled

1 teaspoon dried coriander seeds

1 teaspoon chopped coriander leaves

Freshly cracked black pepper

Lemon juice, to taste

TESTER'S NOTE:
The coriander seeds are important in this dish. I also tried slicing up the broccoli stems first, which made them cook more quickly when I was short on time.

SERVES 4 / TIME: ABOUT 1½ HRS (including roasting the garlic)

Melt the butter in a medium saucepan over medium-high heat. Add the broccoli stems and sear for 8 minutes, until lightly browned, basting continuously by spooning the melted butter over the stems. Add the fresh coriander seeds, bouquets, and stems and continue to baste for another 3 minutes. Slice each stem crosswise into ¼-inch-thick rounds.

Spread a generous amount of the roasted garlic on each broccoli coin, and drape with the lardo so that it melts slightly over the broccoli. Scatter with the dried coriander seeds, coriander leaves, cracked pepper, and a squirt of lemon.

Other Ways to Enjoy Broccoli Scraps

CHILI STIR-FRY

Thinly slice stems crosswise into ¼-inch coins and stir-fry with garlic and chili oil. They stay crunchy even when cooked through.

SHAVE LIKE FINE CHEESE

After peeling off the extremely tough outer layer of the stems, shave the inner core and eat raw.

MAKE SOUP

Make the most of older, limp broccoli stalks and florets by making a pound of broccoli scraps into a smooth cream of broccoli soup. Sauté chopped onion scraps with 3 tablespoons flour and 4 tablespoons (¼ cup) butter base, stirring in one pound of broccoli scraps and simmering for 20 minutes until tender. Puree in the blender.

BRUSSELS SPROUTS

AT THE LATE FALL FARMERS' MARKET I love to see Brussels sprouts' giant clubs with clusters of buds growing up and down the trunk. The entire plant—including the leaves, leaf stalks, and even the inner core of the trunk—is delicious. The Brussels sprout plant begins growing like a cabbage head, but then develops a sturdy central stem that shoots straight up to 3 feet high. Leaves and thick leaf stalks grow out from the stem and, in between them, auxiliary buds form. These auxiliary buds (the sprouts) are harvested, and the rest of the plant, including the large stem, is often left standing in the field. Recently, though, unpackaged Brussels sprouts, still attached to the central stem with the top leaves on, have begun to appear in farmers' markets and supermarket produce sections. Brussels sprouts are hardy in cold weather and can last about two weeks in the refrigerator.

BRUSSELS SPROUTS STEMS & LEAVES WITH WHEY & DILL OIL

This dish shows how a food that is "common" can become uncommon and surprise you with its deliciousness if you think about the whole plant and jazz it up with some fresh herb oil and a bit of briny flavor. It is also one of the ways that I like to make a dressing.

Tip: Instead of always shaking dressing ingredients together in a jar to make the ingredients unite (emulsify) when they don't naturally bond, spoon each of the dressing ingredients around the dish separately so that the natural circles of the herb oil stand out: It looks more beautiful and gives you small bursts of flavor.

1 Brussels sprouts stem, (sprouts and leaves cut off, leaves reserved for below and sprouts for your favorite broiling recipe)

¼ cup (4 ounces) whey (see page 212 to make your own; otherwise use the top layer of liquid from fresh ricotta)

2 tablespoons Dill Oil (page 69)

1 frond fresh dill, chopped

Zest and juice of 1 lemon

1 teaspoon of fresh young kelp, cut into small pieces (optional)

Char the stem: Hold the club-like stem with tongs over a gas flame (or lay flat in a dry cast iron skillet over high heat) and char the entire stem, turning frequently, for 5 minutes. Allow the stem to cool a few seconds, to enable you to handle it with your hands. Wrap the stem in plastic, so that it is enclosed but not too tight. The stem will begin to generate more heat from the core and gently "cook" in its own steam for about 10 minutes, until cool. You will be able to see some steam bubbles collecting inside the wrap during this process. Unwrap the stem and, with a knife, trim off the outer tough layer (save these trimmings for Vegetable Scrap & Peel Stock, page 230). Cut the stem into 1-inch chunks.

Sauté the leaves: The leaves are soft and tender and do not need much time cooking. Tear the leaves into quarters. In a medium saucepan over medium heat, dry sauté the leaves for 3 minutes, until lightly wilted.

To serve: Spoon the whey onto the serving plate. Spoon the oil onto the whey. Since it is not whisked together, the oil will form distinct green bubble-dots against the white whey. Top with the dill fronds, sautéed leaves, stem chunks, lemon zest and juice, and a bit of kelp for added brininess.

TESTER'S NOTES:

I tried to see if I could first cut the giant stem in half as it looked pretty unwieldy, but even hacking at it with a meat cleaver could barely make a dent. So I followed the instructions, and it softened up enough to be able to cut the woody outer wall off with a regular knife, exposing the yummy center. It was crunchy and sweet with a char at the end. It doesn't make a lot of volume, but I think I like it even better than the sprouts. The leaves were also delicious.

SERVES 4 / TIME: 40 MIN (plus 10 min for the dressing)

CABBAGE

A HEAD OF CABBAGE IS BEAUTIFUL, like a wrapped, hefty globe. In cold weather, it is extremely hardy and keeps for months. The centerpiece of the humble cruciferous or brassica family, cabbage is one of the oldest vegetables, an ancestral food that has long been preserved as a staple over long winters and voyages. I love to see a cabbage still sitting in the field after an early snow. I get inspired to use the entire thing.

Asian cabbages, such as bok choy and napa cabbage, are prized for their thick, crunchy, and mild stems, and are great stir-fried in a hot wok. More leafy cabbages, such as mizuna and tatsoi, are also available, and since they do not grow as head cabbages do, there is no core to waste—although they do start to wilt, as leafy greens do.

The parts of the cabbage that are most often discarded are its inner and outermost parts. The bleached center that has not seen the sun is actually quite tender and edible, while the exterior leaves, which are subject to the elements and insect holes, are sweet and mild when cooked.

CABBAGE STEM SALAD WITH BUTTERMILK-HORSERADISH DRESSING

This raw salad is easy to compose. I like to arrange the stems into a beautiful pinwheel shape. For a more filling dish, I serve it atop an 8- to 10-ounce bycatch fish filet, such as sea robin, with additional dressing puddled around it. (For more about bycatch, see Who's the Boss, page 166.)

2 cabbage stems (cauliflower stems also work), lightly trimmed of any extremely fibrous outer peel (reserve for Vegetable Scrap & Peel Stock, page 230)
1 cup Buttermilk-Horseradish Dressing (page 211)
1 teaspoon freshly grated horseradish
Salt and fresh cracked pepper
½ lemon

Using a mandoline, very thinly shave the trimmed cabbage stems lengthwise.

Toss the stem shavings with dressing. Finish with freshly grated horseradish, salt, black pepper, and a squeeze of lemon.

TESTER'S NOTE:
The cabbage and cauliflower stems were shaved so thin, it was like shaved Parmesan, only mild and sweet. I didn't have the fish, so it made a delicious vegetarian dish.

SERVES 4 / TIME: 15 MIN

CABBAGE CORES & LEAVES
IN BROKEN-RICE RISOTTO

This dish makes delicious use of the outermost cabbage leaves as a charred topping, cabbage cores as a crunchy addition to the risotto, and broken rice—a traditionally discarded byproduct of threshing or milling—which takes on a creamy quality when cooked.

4 cups Parmesan Rind Broth (page 213)
    or vegetable or chicken stock

½ head cabbage

4 tablespoons (½ stick) unsalted butter

1 small onion, diced

1 to 2 cabbage or cauliflower cores, diced

Handful of outer leaves from the cabbage,
    at least 2 inches long

Kosher salt

1½ cups broken Arborio rice (see Resources
    for Broken Rice Grits, page 272) or other
    short-grain rice

½ to 1 cup dry white wine or champagne
    (no need to be exact; if you have ¼ cup,
    use it and if you have 1¼ cups, use it)

Grated zest of 1 lemon

4 teaspoons extra virgin olive oil

2 teaspoons fresh thyme leaves

Cracked black pepper

In a medium pan, warm the broth over low heat.

Meanwhile, char the cabbage half: In an ungreased skillet, on a grill, or over an open flame, char the cabbage half for about 3 minutes, until blackened. Remove from the heat and slice against the grain, creating thin shreds of charred and uncharred cabbage.

To cook the rice, melt the butter in a Dutch oven over medium heat. Add the onion, diced cabbage cores, shredded uncharred part of the cabbage half, cabbage leaves, and a pinch of salt and cook for 5 minutes, until softened. Add the rice and stir for 2 minutes to toast the rice. Pour in the wine, reduce the heat to medium-low, and simmer until most of the wine is absorbed. Add ½ cup of the warm broth, stir, and wait for the broth to be absorbed before adding another ½ cup. Continue cooking and adding broth for about 25 minutes, until the rice becomes tender but not mushy.

Remove the rice from the heat, top with the shredded charred cabbage, lemon zest, olive oil, and thyme. Add salt and pepper to taste.

SERVES 4 / TIME: 1 HR

WINTER STUFFED CABBAGE

This is a classic and ultra satisfying meal starting from a whole cabbage. Don't throw out the core, of course; use it for the cabbage core recipes in this book (pp. 43 and 239).

1 savoy cabbage

1 egg

1 teaspoon dried herb, such as thyme or oregano

20 wild juniper berries, crushed and chopped (see p. 246)

1 teaspoon kosher salt

1 pound ground pork

at least 1 cup onion scraps, minced

at least 2 limp carrots, minced

5 tablespoons fresh parsley leaves, chopped

5 slices bacon, diced and cooked until crisp

3 slices stale bread, cut into cubes

Preheat the oven to 350°F.

Bring a large pot of water to a boil. Blanch the cabbage head in the boiling water for 2 minutes (to make the leaves easier to remove). With tongs, remove the cabbage from the water and let it cool slightly, then peel off all the leaves. Return the leaves to the simmering water and cook for about 10 minutes, until just tender, then drain.

In a small bowl, beat the egg with the herb, juniper berries, and salt. With your hands, combine the seasoned egg, pork, onion, carrots, parsley, bacon, and bread in a large bowl until evenly distributed but not overmixed, then form into a ball.

Drape enough of the cabbage leaves to thickly line the bottom and sides of a 14 x 9-inch Dutch oven or casserole dish. Add the stuffing ball and fold the leaves over the top. Cover with a layer of aluminum foil or a lid. Bake for 1 hour, until cooked through.

Serve warm or chilled.

SERVES 5 / ACTIVE TIME: 40 MIN / TOTAL TIME: 1 HR 40 MIN

Other Ways to Enjoy Cabbage Scraps

MAKE A QUICK PICKLED CABBAGE:

Chop cabbage scraps thinly and immerse in a solution of equal parts rice vinegar and sugar. Add celery and carrot scraps if you like for a "scraps slaw." Let it sit for an hour to let the flavors soak in. When serving, grind lots of black pepper over top.

FERMENT INTO SAUERKRAUT:

Shred and sprinkle cabbage scraps with salt (about two teaspoons salt per pound of cabbage), then stuff into a glass jar, pressing them down so that any air bubbles are forced out. Close the lid and store at room temperature, opening it every few days to release air pressure and to sample the contents. When the taste is satisfactory to you, move it to the refrigerator.

DUMPLINGS OR EGGROLLS:

Chop and stir-fry cabbage scraps with a little ground meat, and use as stuffing for dumplings, eggrolls, and savory pancakes. See leftover strategies, page 227, for recipes.

CARROTS

IN 2009, CHEF DANIEL PATTERSON of Michelin-starred Coi, Alta CA, and other Bay Area restaurants, rightly declared, "Carrots are the new caviar." He added, "Revaluing ingredients can lead not only to better food but, equally important in these difficult economic times, to a less costly way of eating." I agree we should value the common carrot—and all its parts—on par with an expensive cut of meat.

What many of us think of as the carrot is actually the root of the carrot plant. But whether steamed, sautéed, pickled, or served raw, each part of the plant can yield delicious results. Carrot tops can have a strong vegetal flavor and rough texture as compared to lettuce, which makes them great for mixing into salads or pureeing. As for the skin, which is also very often discarded, it contains many of the nutrients. And because the skin is so thin, you needn't peel carrots, especially when making a soup, roasting, or juicing them, unless the carrot has been treated heavily with pesticides.

Speaking of carrots and chemicals, I hope it goes without saying that I encourage you to cook with the real thing—not "baby" carrots, which are specially bred to fit industrial cutters and dipped in small amounts of chlorine as an antimicrobial treatment.

CARROT "RAISINS"

This technique turns old, limp carrots into sweet treats. Enjoy them alone as a snack, in granola, or atop a carrot cake or other dessert.

1½ cups sugar
1½ cups water
8 or more unpeeled medium carrots, cut into
    2-inch long barrels about 1 inch in diameter
    (if larger, extend the cooking time)

Use a dehydrator or, alternatively, preheat the oven to 150°F.

Line a baking sheet with parchment paper.

In a medium pot, bring the sugar and water to a boil and simmer until the sugar dissolves. Reduce the heat to medium, add the carrots, and cook for 6 minutes, until the carrots are tender. Let the mixture cool for another 2 minutes, then drain. (Reserve and refrigerate the liquid; it can be used to rehydrate the carrots or to sweeten other dishes.)

Place the carrots in a single layer on the baking sheet. Dehydrate or dry in the oven for 8 to 10 hours, until they are completely dry and no longer feel rubbery. They should look like 1-inch-long batons. The "raisins" can be stored in an airtight container for several months. To use, rehydrate in a little warmed syrup.

TESTER'S NOTE:

The carrots take a while to dehydrate and they reduce in size significantly, so drying a larger amount at one time will be a more efficient use of oven or dehydrator space.

**MAKES APPROXIMATELY ½ CUP DRIED /
ACTIVE TIME: 15 MIN / INACTIVE TIME: 8 TO 10 HRS**

CARROT TOP GRANITA

Who says that vegetables have to be savory? I like to use them to make an icy granita to use as a base for dessert, as in pairing with a light yogurt cloud and some sweet and softened fruits. Because the granita method uses vegetables that are chopped, pureed, and then frozen, it is good for rough or tougher textured vegetables. Carrot tops work beautifully, as do beet tops, wheatgrass, and sorrel. In fact, I use this recipe to make a wheatgrass granita for my Fallen Fruit Dessert, page 95.

2 cups sugar

2 cups water

2 cups chopped carrot tops (or other vegetable tops)

1 cup loosely packed chopped fresh parsley, including stems (if you have less or more parsley, it is fine; don't go out and buy an extra bunch if you only have enough for ½ cup)

¼ cup freshly squeezed lemon juice

3 tablespoons vodka (optional, to keep the granita from turning to ice if you plan to store it longer than a day)

1 cup Whipped Yogurt (page 209)

10–15 Carrot "Raisins" (page 49), or other dehydrated fruit

SERVES 4 /
ACTIVE TIME: 20 MIN /
TOTAL TIME: 3½ HRS (including freezing time)

In a medium pot, combine the sugar and water and bring to a boil, stirring until the sugar is dissolved. Add the carrot tops and parsley, reduce the heat to low, and simmer for 3 minutes, until just cooked. Transfer to a blender, add the lemon juice, and blend for a few minutes to a smooth puree.

Transfer to a shallow metal container at least 8 × 8 × 2 inches, add the vodka (if using), and freeze for 3 to 3½ hours, scraping periodically with a fork so that the granita is evenly frozen.

To serve, crush any remaining lumps in the granita. Fill each of 4 wide shallow bowls with ¼ cup whipped yogurt and dot the yogurt with the carrot raisins. Top each with 3 heaping tablespoons of the granita.

CARROT TOP PESTO

This is a nutty pesto with chewiness and texture. Don't puree it.

1 packed cup finely chopped carrot tops (from about 6 carrots; see Notes)

½ cup packed fresh parsley leaves, wilted is fine

½ cup finely grated Gruyère cheese

½ cup toasted salted walnuts, chopped

Grated zest of 1 lemon

2 tablespoons lemon juice

1 garlic clove, minced

½ cup olive oil

1 teaspoon kosher salt

½ teaspoon sugar (see Notes)

Mix all the ingredients together in a medium bowl.

MAKES ABOUT 2 CUPS / TIME: 15 MIN

CARROT TOP SALSA VERDE WITH PICKLE JUICE

This recipe crosses the definitional line from pesto over to salsa verde. (A pesto uses a nut; a salsa verde has something briny or pickly in it.) The secret ingredient here is pickle juice. I like the strong sourness of the juice left over in the dill pickle jar—not for drinking on its own, but for the sour flavor that balances the carrot tops.

1 packed cup chopped carrot tops (from about 6 carrots; see Note)

¼ cup coarsely chopped pecans

½ cup sour pickle juice

¼ cup sunflower or other neutral oil

Pulse all the ingredients in a blender to a smooth puree.

MAKES 1 CUP / TIME: 10 MIN

NOTE:
Since the carrot top leaves are very flat, a large amount will pack down to a much smaller volume once chopped. The sugar helps to reduce any bitterness from the rough greens.

CAULIFLOWER

CAULIFLOWER IS A MEATY and beautiful vegetable, with enough heft and mildness to eat it whole. You should cherish a cooked hunk of a cauliflower and cut into it with a knife and fork—juicy on the inside and caramelized and crispy on the outside—like a steak.

Derived from the Latin for "stalk cabbage," the cauliflower growing in the field has a flowerhead center surrounded by giant, cabbagey leaves that grow to a foot long or more. Like its close relative, broccoli, only its recognizable flowerhead center is usually sold in markets. Recently, however, "jacket wrapped" cauliflower heads, packaged with their beautifully large leaves, can be found. Still, most of us eat the familiar florets and pitch not only the lovely leaves, but the crunchy, sweet core.

SKILLET-ROASTED CAULIFLOWER CORES & LEAVES WITH BRIE

I've been calling this part of the cauliflower the *stalk* for so long now. But recently, someone told me it is actually the *stem* of the cauliflower, or the *core,* or the *heart.* You can decide for yourself what to call it: maybe just a *part.* It tastes good whatever you decide to call it.

4 cauliflower cores with leaves, trimmed of the very tough outer leaves (but don't discard; reserve them for Vegetable Scrap & Peel Stock, page 230)

3 tablespoons grapeseed oil

2 to 3 tablespoons unsalted butter

4 ounces Brie or Camembert cheese (or even a chunk left over from a cheese plate), cubed

Freshly cracked black pepper

1 teaspoon Maldon salt

Remove the more tender inner layers of leaves from the cauliflower cores and set aside. Cut slits in the cores to expose the surface area of the inner flesh as much as possible.

In a medium saucepan, heat the oil over high heat and sear the cauliflower cores, turning, until each side is golden brown, about 5 minutes. Reduce the heat to medium and add the butter. As the butter is melting, continuously baste the cauliflower by tilting the pan and spooning the butter over the cores for 2 minutes.

Add the Brie and cook until melted. Then add the cauliflower leaves and baste for another 2 minutes, until just cooked. Season generously with a few turns of black pepper and the Maldon salt.

To serve, arrange the cores with the leaves on a plate and spoon the brie-butter over.

SERVES 4 / TIME: 30 MIN

CAULIFLOWER CORE CACIO E PEPE

Cauliflower replaces pasta in this take on the classic *cacio e pepe* (cheese and pepper) pasta. It's an easy recipe when you use a spiralizer, a vegetable spiral slicer that can be used to turn tougher, as well as not-so-tough, parts of vegetables into beautiful noodle-like strands (or other shapes). The addition of green and red pepper seeds adds a little spice.

4 large cauliflower cores, lightly trimmed of the most fibrous outer parts (save for Vegetable Scrap & Peel Stock, page 230)

3 tablespoons unsalted butter

¼ cup leftover seeds and white inner veins from any pepper, such as bell peppers, jalapeños, serranos, poblanos (optional, and no need to be too exacting about the amount. This is waste: If you have it, use it.)

1 teaspoon freshly cracked black pepper

1 cup crème fraîche or heavy cream

½ cup Parmesan Rind Broth (page 213) or other vegetable broth

¾ cup finely grated Parmesan cheese

⅓ cup finely grated Pecorino cheese

½ teaspoon kosher salt

Spiralize the cauliflower cores into a spaghetti shape using the thicker noodle blade of a spiralizer.

In a medium saucepan over medium heat, melt the butter to coat the pan. Add the pepper bits and cracked pepper and sauté for 2 minutes, until the pepper is toasted and aromatic. Mix in the crème fraîche and broth and cook, stirring, for about 5 minutes until the sauce is slightly thickened.

Add the cauliflower spaghetti and cook, stirring occasionally, until just cooked, about 2 minutes. Transfer to a large bowl and immediately add the Parmesan and Pecorino. Toss until the cauliflower is coated and not clumping.

Serve right away, adding more pepper, salt, and cheese, to taste.

SERVES 2 / TIME: 25 MIN

Other Ways to Enjoy Cauliflower Scraps

CAULIFLOWER STEAKS:

Cut the cauliflower head right through the center into thick ½-inch slices. Brown each side in olive oil and then roast in a 400°F oven for 10 minutes, until tender. Serve with pesto, Buttermilk-Horseradish Dressing, or another creamy topping.

CAULIFLOWER SOUP:

In a medium pan, sauté the leftover parts of the cauliflower head with a sliced onion for 5 to 10 minutes, until softened. Add 4 cups chicken stock and 1 cup milk and cook over medium heat for 30 minutes, until tender. Remove from the heat and puree.

CELERY

THE CELERY PLANT GROWS upright with a root ball at the bottom. (Don't confuse the actual root of a celery plant with celeriac, or celery root, which is a different variety that has been bred to grow a large bulbous root without the large "ribs.") The bagged celery that you find in stores usually includes only the elongated ribs (or *stalks*). Botanically, the celery ribs are stalks from which the plant's leaves grow. These leaves are wonderful for flavoring soups and salads and can also serve as an herb.

And the whitish core *bottoms* (not to be overlooked, either) are the stems.

BUTTER-GLAZED CELERY BOTTOMS

Sautéing the celery bottoms using clarified butter allows you to cook at a higher temperature without burning the butter. I serve the softened buttery vegetable bottoms along with fish roe and lots of fresh wild herbs, scattering chive sprouts over the top.

½ cup (1 stick) good-quality unsalted butter

1 shallot, chopped

5 celery bottoms (or other vegetable bottoms such as napa cabbage), 4 to 5 inches long

2 teaspoons lemon juice

2 teaspoons orange juice

1 tablespoon strong-flavored stock or dashi (available from Asian grocery stores or online)

1 teaspoon kosher salt

¼ teaspoon cracked black pepper

3 tablespoons celery leaves, minced chives, and other green herbs (I also used the long shoots of chives because I had them)

3 tablespoons fish roe (optional)

To clarify the butter: In a small pan, melt the butter over low heat, watching as it begins to foam and a clear golden layer of liquid separates, about 12 minutes (see Note). Skim off the top foam and pour the butterfat into a glass container. It may make as much as about ⅓ cup, which is more than enough for the ¼ cup needed for the celery bottoms. Store any extra, including the foam and/or the bottom layer (which can be used as butter for soups, pancakes, and sauces) in the refrigerator for up to 1 month.

To make the celery bottoms: In a small pan, heat ¼ cup clarified butter over medium-low heat. Add the shallot and sauté until softened. Add the celery bottoms and cook, spooning the butter over the ends, for 5 to 7 minutes, until softened. Stir in lemon juice, orange juice, and stock and continue spooning for another minute. Mix in salt, pepper, and herbs and remove from heat. Top with roe for a more substantial dish.

NOTE:
Watch the butter carefully to make sure it doesn't begin to brown. If it does, however, not to worry. You can use it as a deliciously nutty tasting brown butter sauce instead, to be spooned over vegetables, pasta, or fish with a little salt and lemon.

SERVES 2 / TIME: 20 MIN

Other Ways
to Enjoy
Celery Scraps

SOUP BASE:

Use as a flavor base for soups and stews (see Vegetable Scrap & Peel Stock, page 230).

HERB:

Finely chop the leaves and substitute or add to parsley in pasta salads or sandwiches.

ADD CRUNCH:

Dice the thicker, more fibrous parts of the celery and add them to mix some crunch into cold pasta or potato salads.

CELERY SCRAP PESTO

This pesto is simple, boasts good flavor and texture, and keeps well. You can use it as a spread, a dip, or a snack. (Make sure to include the pecans!)

1 cup finely chopped celery leaves
¼ cup chopped celery (inner yellow-white parts are fine also)
⅓ cup chopped pecans
⅓ cup olive oil
1 teaspoon grated lemon zest
¼ teaspoon lemon juice
½ teaspoon kosher salt

In a medium bowl, combine the celery leaves, celery, and pecans. Drizzle with the oil until it is well combined, then mix in lemon zest, juice, and salt.

TESTER'S NOTE:

My knife skills are not so sharp so I pulsed a few times in the food processor, which worked well. The pecans make it really great. We served the pesto with a cold lobster and potato salad and then with Thanksgiving leftovers.

MAKES 2 CUPS / TIME: 15 MIN

FENNEL

ALL PARTS OF THE fennel plant—the seeds, the flowers, the pollen, and the fronds—are aromatic and edible, yet most cookbooks seem to focus only on the bulb. The bulb is actually not a bulb at all, but simply the gathering point of its tightly packed stalks. Both the fronds and stalks are tender and delicious, tasting of mild licorice (which is a popular savory flavor in Denmark). When cooked, the fronds of the fennel plant are even milder.

FENNEL PESTO

This pesto gets a boost from Japanese umeboshi plum paste, which on its own is puckeringly sour. But packed with a mild anise, bread, and herbs, it sings. (Always keep lots of pickly sour things in your refrigerator.)

1 cup fennel stalks (the part between the fronds and the bulb), chopped

¼ cup chopped celery stalks

1 teaspoon kosher salt

⅓ cup neutral oil

¼ cup 1-inch-cubed day-old bread

¼ cup grated **Parmesan**

1 teaspoon pickled plum paste or other sour seasoning

1 squeeze lemon juice

Pulse the fennel and celery stalks in a food processor. Add the salt and then the oil in a slow stream until just mixed. Do not puree. Mix in the bread, Parmesan, and plum paste by hand. Season with a squeeze of lemon.

MAKES 2 CUPS / TIME: 15 MIN

Clockwise from top:
Fennel pesto / Beet Top & Stem Salsa, page 20 / Celery Scrap Pesto, page 58 / Radish Top Chimichurri, page 88 / Carrot Top Salsa Verde with Pickle Juice, page 51

GARLIC, ONIONS, & LEEKS

GARLIC, ONIONS, AND LEEKS are all part of the allium family, which includes hundreds of species and varieties, some sweeter, some with more bite, most having bulbs that last if stored with good ventilation. Although not as perishable as other vegetables, they may not make the grade because they are ugly or misshapen; also, we are accustomed to throwing out the tops and keeping the bottoms (the bulbs).

In the field, garlic bulbs can often become misshapen due to insufficient water or heavy soil. If one clove out of the bunch is malformed, farmers have trouble selling it at markets. They may use it as stock to replant or sell it cheaply as *farmer's garlic*. The rest of the garlic head is perfectly fine. Once garlic gets "old," it also may sprout green shoots. These shoots are tasty to eat as well.

The most perfect young garlic is juicy and mild enough to mince and eat raw. However, the more mature and less perfect cloves can be savored and turn sweet and soft by slow roasting and combining with other flavors.

Like other allium family members (including shallots, green onions, and leeks), the onion is not a root, but a bulb, and grows wild in one form or another in much of the temperate world. It is great cooked or raw and rich in vitamin C, minerals, and trace elements. Onions should not be stored in the refrigerator. Sprouted onions (unlike sprouted potatoes) are fine to eat. Drying garlic and onion scraps can also make them sweeter, with good flavor. Dry overnight at 130°F until brittle. You can use the small dried flakes of onion in dip.

Green onions (aka scallions) last well in the refrigerator, but even when they begin to wilt they can be frozen or dried and made into onion salt. And after the tops are used, the bottoms can be replanted in a pot of soil. The green onion tops will regrow, as will leeks.

Leeks are a member of this family with a very small bulb. Cooks only covet the 5-inch or smaller white stalk at the bottom of the leek plant (recipes calling for leeks' "white and green parts only" mean this). The rest of the two-foot plants, the wide, leafy tops and the roots below, are tossed, presumably because they are large and fibrous. It seems a shame to discard four times the volume of this winter green when the tops are completely edible.

ROASTED UGLY GARLIC

Ugly or not, once slow roasted, this garlic will taste beautifully smooth and sweet.

**1 head garlic, ugly and a bit
   shriveled is fine**
1 teaspoon olive oil

Preheat the oven to 400°F.

Cut a small slice through the top of the garlic, so that the cloves are exposed. Place the garlic on top of a small sheet of aluminum foil and drizzle the top with the oil so that it seeps down between the cloves.

Wrap the garlic in the foil and roast for 45 minutes, until the center is easily pierced with a knife. Slather on crusty bread, crackers, or roasts.

**ACTIVE TIME: 5 MIN /
INACTIVE TIME: 45 MIN**

Other Ways
to Enjoy Leeks

Here are some ideas for
breaking down those unfairly rejected
tough leek greens and roots:

GRILL:

The secret is to slice them
lengthwise and then pre-cook them in
a medium pan with water for
5 minutes to soften them up. Drain
them and store in the refrigerator
for up to 5 days until you are ready to
grill them. Heat a grill to high
(or hold the leeks with tongs over
an open flame on a gas stove);
char until they are slightly blackened
on one side. Serve with horseradish
buttermilk or other dressing.

STIR-FRY:

Break them down by splitting them
vertically and then chopping
them into 1/3-inch pieces, and stir-fry
with minced pork; add rice wine, chili
paste, and garlic and cook for 10 to 15
minutes longer, until softened.

FLASH FRY:

Leek roots are tiny compared to the
aboveground part of the plant.
In a deep pan, heat vegetable oil
until hot and dip the roots in for only
a few seconds. They will taste
like mini crunchy onion threads—
delicious on sandwiches, burgers, or
as salad toppings.

HERBS & GARNISHES

HISTORICALLY, EXOTIC SPICES were luxuries reserved for the rich, whereas native aromatic local plants—i.e., herbs—were for the peasants, particularly as a way of softening and masking less-fresh cuts of meat. Thyme, rosemary, and fennel originated as wild plants on the rocky Mediterranean hillsides. Their highly aromatic fragrances and flavors made simple food delicious, without any further embellishment needed. Herbs also aided in digestion and had therapeutic properties, being high in mineral salts and trace nutrients. Herbs whet the appetite for almost any dish, no matter how frugal.

The woodier herbs, such as thyme, rosemary, and sage, seem more aromatic. Botanically, their leaves are attached to true stems, whereas in the case of more leafy tender green herbs, such as parsley, coriander, dill, and fennel, the leaves are attached to leaf stalks. The more tender green "leaf stalks" are easy to use by chopping more finely. Herbs with woodier true stems are better for using in stocks and stuffings, with roasts, and hanging in bunches to dry because of their woody structure.

I must always have Herbs (pronounced with the *H*). By a Herb, I mean almost any small green that is not a vegetable. Not just parsley, thyme, and rosemary, but also nasturtium leaves, upland cress, dandelion greens, and chickweed (see Wild Herbs Glossary, page 269). Some people don't understand why I'm crazy about Herbs because they think they are only good as some kind of "garnish." Garnishes are often not used well; think of an orange slice or some curly parsley sprig that looks like it's been used over and over. But a true garnish is the finishing to the flavors of a chunk of vegetable or protein. Without the Herb, it is like writing a letter and forgetting to sign it.

Dishes loaded with salt, pepper, and sugar alone are *seasoned*, but don't always have real *flavor*. Start using more Herbs for flavor and don't stick to only one kind of Herb. If it is not written in the recipe, you can still try another. If the recipe says use dill with salmon, that's fine. But why not use other ones if that's what you have? Maybe thyme, lambsquarters, fennel, and lemon balm (as in Scraped Salmon Tartare on the Bone, page 169). Or use dill with Brussels sprouts (in Brussels Sprout Stems & Leaves with Whey & Dill, page 39).

Try just a little at first, and if you don't like the taste, you can always just spit it out. It's not going to ruin your meal if you have extra thyme or less rosemary or put in some chopped parsley or fennel tops.

Herbs don't have to be piled up high on a plate as a "salad." They are part of the dressing that must be on every dish; otherwise the dish would feel naked. Herbs can give energy and balance to fatty meat or fish to make the dish refreshing. Adding fresh Herbs is better than grinding pepper all the time, and they can have a similar effect of adding a bit of heat.

I divide Herbs into two different types: The first are the strong Herbs that are often cooked and that you can put on the grill, like thyme and rosemary. The other type includes leafy, green, and tender Herbs that add refreshment and lightness, like young sprouts and shoots of vegetables, chickweed, purslane, lambsquarters, and spruce tips. Because these are fresh I want them to be local and seasonal (some Herbs' lives are very fleeting), changing the mix when nature changes.

There is such a variety among land Herbs: I like dill flowers, nasturtium, rosemary, parsley, chervil, lovage, upland cress, purslane, flowering mint, sorrels of all kinds, mustard greens, dandelion greens, cattail, amaranth, onion shoots, young yarrow. I always, always have to have fresh and dried Herbs in the pantry. They are more important to me than spices.

So instead of throwing Herbs into the bottom of the refrigerator to turn moldy and slimy, use what you need fresh and then hang the rest up to dry. You can use the dried parts in a nice tea (see Tea from Scraps, page 223). Having a couple pots of Herbs indoors also saves a lot of waste since you need only pick what you need that day.

THYME SCRAPS OIL

Herb oils add both depth and nuance to dishes, and they are so simple to make. Use leftover packets and odd bits of herbs. Thyme oil is essential to the Wilted Romaine Cream Sauce recipe (page 75), and complements many other proteins: fish and meat as well as vegetable dishes.

1 bunch (¼ cup) thyme leaves and parts
1 cup neutral oil, such as grapeseed or safflower

In a blender, combine the thyme and oil at high speed for a few seconds, until just turning green. Strain into a small bowl through a fine mesh strainer lined with cheesecloth. Keep the strainer in the bowl and refrigerate overnight to let the thyme slowly infuse into the oil. The oil should become a brilliant green. Store in a dark container in the refrigerator for up to a month.

MAKES 1 CUP / ACTIVE TIME: 5 MIN / TOTAL TIME: OVERNIGHT

DILL OIL

Dill is not as strongly flavored as thyme, although still nicely aromatic. So you can use a greater proportion of dill scraps, wilt, and stems here without requiring as long an infusion. This oil is a very important element of the Whey and Dill Oil dressing used in the Brussels sprout recipe on page 39; it works as well with fish, in a rice salad, or with eggs.

½ cup neutral oil
1 cup fresh dill scraps, (stems, wilted fronds) plus a fresh frond for garnish
1 teaspoon vinegar
Pinch of sugar

Combine all of the ingredients in a blender and puree until thoroughly mixed. Store in the refrigerator for up to a week.

MAKES ABOUT 1½ CUPS / TIME: 5 MIN

WILTED HERB BUTTER WITH GARLIC

High-quality butter is very important in Denmark and is commonly flavored with herbs and grasses, then smeared over thick bread.

½ cup (1 stick) unsalted butter, softened at room temperature
¼ cup wilted chopped parsley leaves and stems
½ to 1 cup finely chopped kale or beet stems
¼ cup or more chopped thyme stems and leaves (no need to measure exactly, but the more herbs, the stronger the flavor; you can also substitute rosemary or sage)
2 teaspoons grated lemon zest
2 cloves garlic, chopped
½ teaspoon kosher salt

In a medium bowl, combine all the ingredients and beat with a fork. Let stand at least 2 hours in the refrigerator to let the flavors infuse. Spread over warm charred or toasted bread. Refrigerate leftovers for up to 5 days.

TESTER'S NOTE:
I tried some store-bought herb butter to compare—this "make it yourself from scraps" version had so much more flavor. There was no comparison.

MAKES ABOUT 1½ CUPS / TIME: 15 MIN

KALE

KALE IS PART OF the same family of large *brassica*-related plants as cabbage, broccoli, and cauliflower. While cauliflower is known as "stalk cabbage," kale is known as "leaf cabbage." Indeed, the leaves of the kale plant have long been used as a hardy cold-weather vegetable in winter dishes when nothing else was available. Today there is something of a renaissance of kale, with many leafy varieties available, such as baby kale, curly kale, and lacinato or dinosaur kale, all of which hold up well in cold weather, in the refrigerator, and in the freezer. In the center of some mature kale leaves runs a rib, which is often dismissed as tough and stringy. But these ribs are perfectly fine to eat; they simply need to be cooked longer to give them time to soften.

KALE PULP PASTA WITH TORN KALE SAUCE

3 cups all-purpose flour, plus additional for dusting
¼ cup Kale Powder (page 73)
1 teaspoon kosher salt
3 whole large eggs plus 3 yolks, beaten
1 tablespoon olive oil
Semolina flour, for dusting
Torn Kale Sauce (page 73)
**Fresh herbs, crumbled feta cheese, nuts, and freshly
    cracked black pepper, for serving**

In a medium bowl, combine the flour, kale powder, and salt. On a lightly floured surface, make a well out of the flour mixture and pour the eggs and oil into the center. Gradually incorporate the sides of the well into the eggs, working in more flour until the dough is moist but no longer wet. Knead the dough by hand for about 20 minutes, until firm to the touch, adding flour if the dough is too sticky and drops of water if too dry. (Or use a food processor or standing mixer with a dough hook and knead for 5 to 10 minutes.) Wrap the dough in plastic and chill in the refrigerator for at least 30 minutes.

Dust 2 baking sheets liberally with semolina flour. Cut the dough into quarters and press flat.

Roll each quarter (keeping the remaining quarters of dough wrapped) several (about 3) times through a pasta rolling machine, starting at the thickest setting, and adjusting to progressively thinner settings, until ⅛ inch thick (on most pasta machines, either the last or second-to-last setting is best).

Cut long strips of pasta about ¾-inch wide. You may leave them long or cut into diagonal or other shorter lengths. Gently toss the cut pasta in the semolina flour so they stay separated and coated.

Repeat with the remaining dough quarters.

Bring a large pot of salted water to a rolling boil. Add the pasta and cook for 90 seconds, until still chewy. Drain.

In a large bowl, toss the pasta with the kale sauce. Taste for seasoning. Finish with herbs, feta, nuts, and a few turns of freshly cracked black pepper.

**SERVES 4 / ACTIVE TIME: 1 HR /
INACTIVE TIME: 30 MIN**

KALE POWDER

In general, powders are a great way to preserve and concentrate flavors and waste less. If you get used to dehydrating wasted parts and set up a storage pantry to keep them, you can grind and make your powders with minimal time before using. Experiment with your powders as if they were an edible chemistry set. Kale powder can be used as a vegetable spice to sprinkle over potatoes, chips, salads, and pasta.

½ pound kale pulp (about a ½-gallon bag), left over from home juicing or from a local juice bar

Use a dehydrator, or if you don't have one, preheat the oven to the lowest temperature, preferably 110°F.

Spread the pulp out in a thin layer on a flat baking sheet or screen. Dehydrate at 150°F for 4 hours, or overnight in the oven at 110°F, until completely dry and crispy.

Store in an airtight container without direct exposure to light. When ready to use, grind in a spice or coffee grinder into a fine powder.

**MAKES ABOUT 1 CUP /
ACTIVE TIME: 15 MIN /
TOTAL TIME: 4 HRS or overnight
(depending on your dehydration process)**

TORN KALE SAUCE

3 tablespoons sunflower or other neutral oil

2 packed cups lacinato kale leaves (the soft part of the leaf torn away from and removing the middle rib; save the ribs for the Kale Chips, at right, or Wrinkled Berry Salsa with Herb & Kale Stems, page 108)

2 cloves garlic, minced

1 cup crème fraîche

¼ cup Parmesan Rind Broth (page 213) or vegetable broth

2 tablespoons freshly squeezed lemon juice

1 teaspoon kosher salt

1 lightly packed cup fresh herbs, I used wild herbs (see page 66) like lambsquarters and shiso, roughly chopped

1 tablespoon chopped walnuts or pecans

1 cup crumbled feta cheese

In a large saucepan, heat the oil over medium-high heat. Add the kale leaves and garlic and sauté for 1 minute, until the kale is wilted. Stir in the crème fraîche, broth, lemon juice, and salt. Finish by adding a flavorful mixing of herbs, nuts, and cheese over the top of the dish.

4 SERVINGS or approximately 2 cups / TIME: 15 MIN

WILTED KALE OR CHARD CHIPS

1 bunch wilted (or not) kale or other hardy vegetable leaves (see Note), chopped into 2-inch pieces

2 tablespoons grapeseed oil

½ teaspoon kosher salt

Preheat the oven to 350°F. Line a baking sheet with parchment paper.

In a large bowl, mix the leaves with the oil until coated. Sprinkle with salt and spread on the baking sheet so they don't overlap. Bake for 15 to 20 minutes, rotating the sheet after 10 minutes, until the kale edges are just browned. Let cool.

NOTE:

If using chard or mature kale, remove the thick center rib, but do not discard; use for powder or for the Wrinkled Berry Salsa with Herb & Kale Stems (page 108).

SERVES 4 / TIME: ABOUT 30 MIN

LETTUCE

LETTUCE IS LIKELY ONE of the most wasted vegetables in the United States, amounting to 1 billion pounds of uneaten salads a year. Whether it's the outer leaves—which are often rough, torn, or have spots—or the white-ish, crunchy bottoms, much of the plant is considered undesirable. What's more, lettuce leaves can have a shorter shelf life than other vegetables, as they tend to wilt, cling together, and become slimy and unpalatable. (They will, however, stay fresh longer when wrapped in paper towels to reduce moisture and stored in a rigid plastic container.) But even when leaves start to lose their structure and become soft and yellowish, they can still be resurrected.

Although I like to use the whole plant, the romaine lettuce roots are so tiny that I gave up on my goal of digging them all out from Comeback Farm's lettuce row. Sometimes it *is* too much to use the whole...and the roots can just return to nourish the ground where they lie.

SEARED ROMAINE LETTUCE BOTTOMS

I made this at ACME restaurant and it turned out to be so popular that we ended up with too many wilting lettuce leaves left over. So I started using the lettuce to make Wilted Romaine Cream Sauce (at right) to go with the bottoms.

2 tablespoons grapeseed or other light vegetable oil

4 (3- to 4-inch) romaine lettuce bottoms, trimmed of brown-orange edges and cut flat on the top so they can sit in the pan

4 teaspoons lemon juice

1 tablespoon kosher salt

¼ cup Wilted Romaine Cream Sauce (at right)

3 tablespoons Thyme Scraps Oil (page 69)

Heat the grapeseed oil in a large saucepan over high heat, until sizzling but not smoking. Add the lettuce bottoms, cut sides down, and sear for 3 minutes, until the bottoms are caramelized and golden brown. Remove from the pan and sprinkle with the lemon juice and salt.

To serve, spoon the sauce on each of 4 plates and arrange a seared bottom on top. Drizzle with the thyme oil and serve.

SERVES 4 (add additional bottoms for more servings) / TIME: 10 MIN

WILTED ROMAINE CREAM SAUCE

This sauce is so adaptable for use in a number of vegetable scraps recipes, including the Butter-Glazed Celery Bottoms (page 56), and as a dip for crudités, lettuce wraps, with pork chops, and to top a salad. Substitute freely in any recipe calling for "creamy Ranch dressing."

2 tablespoons grapeseed or other neutral vegetable oil
2 small shallots, roughly sliced
1 small yellow onion, diced small
2 cloves garlic, smashed
1 cup heavy cream
12 damaged whole romaine lettuce leaves (old, torn, and wilted is good)
1 teaspoon kosher salt
1 tablespoon lemon juice, plus 1 lemon for squeezing

Heat the oil in a medium saucepan over medium-high heat. Add the shallots, onion, and garlic and sauté for about 7 minutes, until the onions are lightly browned. Deglaze the pan with the cream, and cook for 1 minute, scraping up any bits on the bottom of the pan.

Pour the sauce into a blender. Add the lettuce leaves and puree until very smooth. Season with salt and lemon juice. The sauce can be stored in the refrigerator for up to a week.

After pouring the dressing, top with a drizzle of Thyme Scraps Oil.

TESTER'S NOTE:
Adding Thyme Scraps Oil (page 69) made this sauce's flavor really fantastic.

MAKES 3 CUPS / TIME: 15 MIN

Other Ways to Enjoy Lettuce Scraps

LETTUCE CUPS:
Large outer leaves from whole heads can be used as wraps for leftover cooked meats, such as bacon, shredded chicken, ground beef, and herbs. Just avoid ingredients that are watery or above room temperature.

TACO TOPPING:
Shred extra leaves and use as a side or topping for tacos or other Mexican dishes.

SOUP:
Chop wilted lettuce or lettuce scraps and add to a potato-based soup during the last 10 minutes of cooking, then puree.

Lettuce is
likely one of
the most wasted
vegetables
in the United
States . . .
amounting to
1 billion pounds
of uneaten
salads a year.

PEAS

PEAS REMIND ME OF SPRING. Each part of the young plant—the tendrils, the stem, the leaves—tastes fresh and light and juicy. That's why I always search for the whole pea plant, which is actually an edible shoot. Other than snow pea or snap pea pods, the pods of English or garden peas are usually considered too tough and thrown out, leaving just the seeds or what we call *peas*. But the rest of the plant, which can grow to 5 feet high, is delicious.

PEA SHOOTS

THE SHOOTS of the pea plant, what is usually thrown out in the field, can be found in Asian grocery stores. Chop and stir-fry pea shoots (also known as *dou miao*)—the leaves, stems, and tendrils of the young pea plant—with or without garlic, add a little broth at the end until the color turns deep green and leaves are tender but not mushy. Add bamboo shoots or mushrooms and serve as a side dish.

CHILLED PEA PLANT SOUP
WITH DAIKON-PEA DUMPLINGS

This is a raw soup that must be thoroughly blended to a fine puree and then strained. The dumplings complete the dish for a fresh and satisfying springtime meal.

4 cups pea shoots and pods, available where fresh peas are in season, plus a few pea shoots for garnish (see Note)

¼ cup water

1 teaspoon rice wine vinegar

1 squeeze lemon juice

⅛ teaspoon kosher salt

Herb oil

Daikon-Pea Dumplings (at right)

Grapeseed oil, for serving

In a blender, puree the shoots and pods with the water. Strain the puree to be sure the strings and fibrous parts are removed, especially if you are including pea pods.

In a medium bowl, combine the pea puree, vinegar, lemon juice, and salt. Refrigerate for at least 15 minutes or until chilled, and drizzle with an herb oil of choice. I like to use tarragon (using the Thyme Scraps Oil recipe on page 69).

To serve: Arrange 5 or 6 dumplings in the bottom of a bowl. Ladle the chilled pea pod soup around the dumplings until reaching halfway up the sides of the dumplings. Finish with a strand or two of pea shoots and a drizzle of grapeseed oil.

NOTE:

Reserve the peas for the dumplings; all the other parts have a fresh pea taste so you can also use some of the tender shoots or pods as garnish.

SERVES 4 / TIME: 1 HR 15 MIN

DAIKON-PEA DUMPLINGS

These light and delicious dumplings use shaved radish as wrappers, and peas, pea vegetation, and herbs as filling.

Wrappers

1 large daikon radish, at least 3 inches in diameter, peeled (don't throw away the peels; save for pickles, see Other Ways to Enjoy Radishes, page 87)

½ lemon

About 2 tablespoons grapeseed or other neutral oil

About 1 tablespoon kosher salt

Filling

½ cup chopped pea shoots or pods

2 cups shelled peas

¼ cup loosely packed fresh mint leaves

¼ cup loosely packed fresh flat-leaf parsley leaves

2 tablespoons minced fresh chives

¼ cup grapeseed oil

2 tablespoons freshly squeezed lemon juice

1 teaspoon kosher salt

For the wrappers: With a mandoline, slice the radish crosswise as thinly as possible, until you have 25 ultra-thin circular slices. The slices must be thin enough to be pliable, like a dumpling wrapper. Lay them flat and separate on an 8 × 11-inch baking sheet lined with parchment paper.

Partially squeeze the lemon half, and lightly rub over each slice. Dab a small amount of oil and a pinch of salt on each slice. Let marinate for at least 20 minutes in the refrigerator.

For the filling: In a food processor, pulse the pea shoots, shelled peas, mint, parsley, chives, oil, lemon juice, and salt to a coarse blend. Add additional salt and lemon, to taste. The filling can be made a day ahead.

To assemble: Spoon 1 teaspoon of the pea puree into the middle of each daikon round and fold the daikon wrapper up around the filling, gently twisting the wrapper at the top to close, creating a little parcel.

MAKES 25 DUMPLINGS, 4 SERVINGS / TIME: 1 HR

POTATOES

THE HUMBLE POTATO IS the number one vegetable crop in the United States and, not surprisingly, high on the list of wasted foods in North America. Much of this waste occurs prior to distribution, because potatoes are susceptible to discoloration of the skin and to cavities on the inside. Since the potato is the underground tuber (not the root) of the plant, it is actually a bump or swelling that stores the plant's nutrients (mostly in the skin) for the leafy greens that grow above ground. (This aboveground part of the plant contains solamine and is thus inedible.) To inhibit green growth, store potatoes in a pantry, away from light. Green potatoes or green growth emerging from potatoes should be discarded.

Another Way to Use Potatoes

BUBBLE & SQUEAK:

In the United Kingdom it is popular to enjoy a proper leisurely Sunday lunch with a roast, vegetable, and potatoes (mashed, roasted, or boiled). The following Monday for supper, the leftovers are combined into a dish known as bubble and squeak: Mix leftover potatoes with some chopped cabbage or other chopped, cooked vegetable. In a medium saucepan, sauté sliced onions in olive oil with a dash of salt and pepper. Mix the onions into the leftover potatoes, along with any vegetables, or shredded or chopped bite size pieces of meat. Form into pancakes and fry in vegetable oil until browned on one side, then flip like a burger and fry until golden on the other side.

See the chapter on leftovers (page 227) for more ways to use potatoes.

SMOKY POTATO SCRAP BROTH WITH POTATO NOODLES

This soup takes on the flavor of smoky baked potato skins (and other vegetable peels), and its noodles are actually the rest of the peeled potato, spiralized.

2 organic russet potatoes, scrubbed

4-inch piece (½ ounce) dried konbu

½ cup loosely packed mixed seaweeds, such as dulse, arame, and hijiki

1 ounce applewood smoked dulse (optional)

Generous ¼ cup hickory wood chips, toasted for 30 minutes at 350°F

1 cup fresh shiitake stems or other mushroom scraps

1 cup vegetable scraps, such as root vegetable peels, leek tops, and onion ends

1½ cups rice wine vinegar

1 teaspoon fish sauce

Kosher salt

2 cloves garlic, finely minced

1 loosely packed cup of any herb scraps, such as fennel, or dill stems and fronds

¼ cup lemon juice

Grated lemon zest, spruce tips, and sea herbs, for serving (optional)

Preheat the oven to 375°F.

Peel the potatoes and spread the peels evenly on an 8 × 11-inch baking sheet. Bake for 25 minutes, until dry, shriveled, and browned. Set the peels aside.

Meanwhile, bring a large pot of water (3 quarts) to a boil. Use a spiralizer to cut the peeled potatoes into long strands. Plunge them into the boiling water and cook for 1 to 2 minutes, until just softened. Remove the potatoes with a slotted spoon (but continue to boil the water) and transfer to a large bowl of cold water to soak to keep them from turning brown.

Add the konbu, seaweeds, dulse (if using), wood chips, and mushroom and vegetable scraps to the boiling water, reduce the heat, and simmer for about 45 minutes, until the broth is dark and smoky.

While the broth is simmering, make the noodle marinade: In a large bowl, combine the rice wine vinegar, fish sauce, 3 cups water, and 1 tablespoon salt. Drain the potato noodles, add to the marinade, and let marinate for 30 minutes or more while you work on the rest of the recipe.

Remove the smoky broth from the heat and add the reserved baked potato peels, garlic, and herb scraps and let infuse for 30 minutes. Strain the broth through a strainer. Add the lemon juice and 2 teaspoons salt.

To serve: Drain the noodles and portion them equally into individual bowls, ladling in the strained broth. Finish with a pinch of lemon zest, spruce tips, and sea herbs if you like.

SERVES 4 / ACTIVE TIME: 45 MIN / INACTIVE TIME: 1 HR 15 MIN

Smoky Potato
Scrap Broth with
Potato Noodles,
seaweeds, and
spruce tips

RADISHES

LIKE MANY VEGETABLES, THE radish is the root of a plant. The most familiar of its many varieties is the crunchy red or pink table radish, which is often eaten raw, either whole or shaved. When red radishes are young and crisp, I eat them raw with the tops still attached. (They're especially delicious dipped in an oyster-flavored mayonnaise.) When radishes become larger and more mature, however, their tops and peels are often considered waste. And when they crack or go limp and rubbery in the vegetable bin, they end up discarded—but not by us!

Other Ways to Enjoy Radishes

MAKE DAIKON RADISH PEEL PICKLES
(a treat in regional Chinese cuisine):

Cut radish peels 3 to 4 inches long and marinate in $1/2$ cup dark malty Chinese black vinegar, $1/2$ cup light soy sauce, and $1/3$ cup sugar for at least 2 hours. Store in the refrigerator for up to one week.

COOK LARGE RADISHES,
such as daikon, that have become limp or soft, to bring out their juicy character:

In a medium pot, sauté about 1 pound of 1-inch-thick radish slices in a neutral oil for about 5 minutes, until lightly browned. Add 1 cup strong dashi (bonito flakes and water), 2 tablespoons sugar, and $1 1/2$ tablespoons soy sauce and simmer for 10 minutes, until the radishes are cooked through and softened. Serve as a side dish with meat and steamy rice.

DRY RADISH POWDER:

Slice up shriveled, fully dried radishes and grind into a powder to use as a substitute for garlic powder.

RADISH SCRAPS
CHIMICHURRI

No nuts (pesto), no briny vinegar
(salsa verde)… not a "salad,"
so technically it's a "scraps"
chimichurri from radish tops.
Good on its own or with toast or
crackers.

**1 packed cup chopped red radish
tops (or white turnip tops)**
**½ cup ⅓-inch chopped radishes
(ugly is fine); use a little more or
less, depending what you have**
¼ cup feta cheese
¼ cup grapeseed oil
Juice of ½ lemon
**½ teaspoon sugar or to taste
(see Note)**

In a medium bowl, combine the
radish tops, radishes, feta, oil,
lemon juice, and sugar.

NOTE:
If using daikon radish or other
more spicy/bitter tops, adding
sugar will tame the heat.

MAKES 2 CUPS / TIME: 15 MIN

ON VEGETABLE PEELS & PESTICIDES

According to the Environmental Working Group, the following produce have been found to contain the highest levels of pesticide residue, which often concentrates in the skins. Thus buying organic makes more sense when cooking with these ingredients, particularly the peels.

Strawberries
Apples
Nectarines
Peaches
Celery
Grapes
Cherries
Spinach
Tomatoes
Sweet Bell Peppers
Cherry Tomatoes
Cucumbers
Hot Peppers

3

FRUIT

I like ugly fruit. I am not talking about rotten fruit, but overripe fruit whose flavors have had time to become concentrated.

WHETHER YOU'RE USING overripe fruit for granitas, cocktails, or sauces; whether you are roasting, baking, or fermenting, fruit that is soft, getting mushy or wrinkly, or is anything less than "perfect" can be exciting and delicious.

That is why I find it especially tragic that more than 6 billion pounds a year of fresh produce goes unharvested in the United States. Why? Mostly due to demand for perfect specimens, but also due to large-scale mechanical harvesting, which passes over some edible produce while picking and bruising others during processing. Some fields are even left to fallow with fruit and vegetables rotting. A *walk by,* also known as a *pre-harvest shrink,* occurs when the prices that a crop can command are so low (due to oversupply or decreased demand) that they do not even cover the cost of labor and resources to harvest and get the crop to market.

Most people I meet think of fruit as something to eat out of hand or in a pie. I agree that there is almost nothing that beats picking a fruit out of an orchard and eating it right there. But there are so many other ways to enjoy fruits, many of which may taste even "fruitier" than eating it raw from a tree. And you can use the sweetness of fruit instead of sugar to give your cooking more depth. Just as vegetables can be used for sweets and desserts, fruits can be used for savory dishes with fantastic results. Fatty meats like ribs become mouthwatering with a fruity sauce. See Pork Ribs with Overripe-Pear Barbecue Sauce on page 123.

A

BETTER WAY

ACCORDING TO CHIP PAILLEX, who owns and operates a number of farms in New Jersey, there has to be a better way. Says Paillex, "There is no reason why anyone should be faced with hunger in New Jersey, the Garden State. Plenty of food can be rescued from farms and supermarkets. We just need access and hands to harvest and a method of distribution."

America's Grow-a-Row, Paillex's nonprofit organization, relies on volunteers to harvest crops and deliver them to food banks. They also host urban youth and low-income communities to come harvest fresh food for themselves. Chip's volunteers glean old fruit under the trees at his orchards as well as at neighboring farms for use in food banks and kitchens. Fresh fallen plums and apples cover the ground with bounty begging to be devoured.

Left: Apple wedges for drying in the Fallen Fruit Dessert (page 95).

APPLES

ALTHOUGH YOU CAN STILL FIND the wild species of some crabapples, the familiar large fleshy apple has been cultivated around the world for centuries. In 2016 more than 6.5 million tons of apples are expected to be produced worldwide, with 4.5 million tons in the United States alone. The cores and skins of the apple are often discarded but are completely edible. In fact, botanically speaking, the apple has no hard core; the inner area is known as the *pericarp*. The seeds do contain trace amounts of cyanide (700 mg per kilo) and if consumed in large amounts (100 grams) are toxic. Thus, this is the only element of the apple to be avoided.

Apples store well. When individually wrapped in newspaper and kept in cold storage (35° to 40°F), they can last the winter. But one bruised apple in a bin can spread rot to other apples and should be removed.

FALLEN FRUIT DESSERT

Every autumn in Denmark I would walk around the apple orchards where fruit was scattered all over the ground. It made me hungry, and I couldn't help picking some up to bite into them. I wanted to capture this feeling for other people, so I made a dessert I call Fallen Fruit.

It's simple: Apple wedges, dried until they turn chocolate brown, develop intense flavor. Set them on a cool green ice granita, and they look like fruit that has just fallen to the ground.

3 cups cider

At least 8 overripe ugly, bruised, or partially used apples (and other hard fruit, such as pears or plums), unpeeled, cut into wedges, or larger apples cut into eighths

1 cup water (optional)

1 cup sugar (optional)

1 quince, cut into chunks (optional)

Wheatgrass granita (substitute wheatgrass and sorrel for the carrot tops in **Carrot Top Granita**, page 50)

½ cup frozen spruce tip needles (see page 246 for foraging tips)

Drying apples intensifies the apple flavor. Use a dehydrator at 135°F, or preheat the oven at the lowest setting.

Bring the cider to a boil in a large saucepan. Add the apple wedges, reduce the heat to low, and simmer for 8 minutes, until just tender, not falling apart.

Spread the mixture on a sheet pan and dehydrate at 135°F (or in the oven) for 12 hours, until soft. Keep refrigerated until ready to use (no more than 2 days).

Make a quince paste, if you like: Bring the water and sugar to a boil over medium-high heat. Add the quince, reduce the heat, and simmer for 30 minutes, or until very soft. Transfer to a blender and puree.

To serve: Spoon the granita into individual bowls, add the dried fruit with a spoon of the quince puree, and scatter the spruce needles over top.

SERVES 4 / ACTIVE TIME: 30 MIN / TOTAL TIME: 12 HRS

Other Ways to Use Apple Scraps

APPLE SCRAP STOCK

Sarah Villamere, ingenious pastry chef, formerly of Raymonds in Newfoundland, uses this stock as a base syrup for jellies and drinks. And she uses the leftover pulp in her Apple Scrap Cake (at right). Collect the apple cores over time and keep them in the freezer until you have enough.

20 or more apple cores
¾ cup sugar
½ cup dried apple peel (optional)

In a large pot, cover the apple cores with water and bring to a simmer over medium-low heat, adding the sugar and apple peel (if using). (Tip: To concentrate the flavor, lay a piece of parchment on the water's surface.) Cook over low heat for about 1½ hours, until the apple cores are falling apart and mushy.

Strain through a strainer lined with cheesecloth into a pot. To extract as much stock as possible, tie the ends of the cloth together over a wooden spoon and suspend it over the pot. Place the entire contraption in the refrigerator overnight for the liquid to drip into the bowl.

The next morning, press down on the solids to extract more juices. You should have about 1½ cups fragrant pink apple stock. Open up the cheesecloth and find the thickened apple pulp. Remove the seeds and woody bits.

MAKES 1½ CUPS STOCK and about 1 cup packed pulp
ACTIVE TIME: 30 MIN / TOTAL TIME: 12 HRS or overnight

SARAH'S APPLE SCRAP CAKE

½ cup (1 stick) unsalted butter, softened
1 cup packed brown sugar
2 eggs
1 teaspoon vanilla extract
1¼ cups pulp from Apple Scrap Stock (at left)
2 cups all-purpose flour
2 teaspoons baking powder
½ teaspoon baking soda
1 teaspoon ground cinnamon
½ teaspoon ground ginger
1 teaspoon salt

Preheat the oven to 350°F.

Cream the butter and sugar in a large bowl until smooth. Add the eggs and vanilla, followed by the apple scrap pulp. Sift the flour, baking powder, baking soda, cinnamon, ginger, and salt together in a medium bowl. In batches, mix the dry ingredients into the batter.

Transfer the batter to an 8-inch round cake pan. Bake for 30 to 40 minutes, until the cake is golden brown. Let cool.

SERVES 9 TO 10 /
ACTIVE TIME: 20 MIN /
INACTIVE TIME: 30 TO 40 MIN

APPLE SCRAP VINEGAR

6 (or more) apple cores and peels

This is a quick and easy starter version. Leave the cores and peels on a covered plate at room temperature for one day, until they start to turn brown. In a gallon jar, combine the cores and peels with enough water to reach 2 inches from the top. Add 1½ cups sugar. Cover the jar with cheesecloth and store in a warm dark closet. (If you are going to be using more apples over the next week, continue to add peels and cores.) Check after a few days to see if the water is cloudy and a grayish scum has formed on top. This is part of the fermentation process. It should be ready in about 4–6 weeks and will get sharper the longer you leave it. Strain and store in the refrigerator in a clear glass container.

MAKES 1 QUART /
ACTIVE TIME: 20 MIN /
TOTAL TIME: ABOUT 1 MONTH

Other Ways
to Enjoy Old Apples,
Apple Peels, and
Apple Cores

APPLE TEA:

Add the peels of two red apples
to 3 cups water in a small saucepan
and bring to a boil. Turn off the
heat, add a cinnamon stick, and steep
for about 12 minutes, until the
water turns red and the apple flavors
the water. Strain.

APPLE PEEL POWDER:

Dry apple peels for 24 hours
in a 115°F dehydrator, or bake for
3 hours in a 225°F oven until
completely dry. Store in an airtight
container. Grind and use as a
flour to add to pancakes.

APPLE SCRAP SAUCE:

Quarter 5 or more mushy old
unpeeled organic apples. In a large
pot, cover the apple chunks with
water and cook over medium heat
until they are so soft that they are
falling apart, about 45 minutes. Let
cool slightly and remove the seeds.
Transfer to a food processor and
pulse until pureed. (You can make it
into a thicker spread by draining in a
small mesh strainer to remove some of
the liquid, then cook the pulp longer
over low heat.) Add cinnamon and
nutmeg to taste.

BANANAS

AMERICANS CONSUME MORE THAN 3 BILLION pounds of bananas a year; about 12 percent of that weight is in the banana peel, which is in fact edible when cooked until tender. Bananas grow in upside-down clusters on a 16-foot-high plant that looks big enough to be a tree, but it is actually a giant herbaceous plant. Bananas are a staple food crop in the Southern Hemisphere, particularly in Southeast Asia and Latin America, where they grow several different varieties and which they eat fried, boiled, baked, and raw. Most people eat only the inside, which is called the *pulp,* but the skin and the blossoms (or *hearts*) are delicious, and the leaves can be used to wrap steamed food or as a waterproof serving dish. A classic Thai dish is minced chicken and banana blossom salad. Banana works well in other savory dishes, too. I like to pair the sweet flavor of the overripe fruit with salted cabbage, searing them together in a cast iron pan and adding some salt.

Most bananas in American grocery stores are from one cultivar and are shipped underripe. On a visit to our local ShopRite, we found they were only selling green bananas. When we asked the produce manager if they had ripe bananas, he hospitably escorted us to the back storage area where they had boxes and boxes of perfect yellow bananas. He told us that they had been removed from the sales display because no one would buy perfect yellow bananas, only green underripe ones. (Admirably, the store had arranged for them to be distributed as animal feed and not sent to a landfill.) Despite many people's aversion to them, browning bananas are fine to eat. Spoiled or bruised parts simply need to be cut away. And if bananas become overripe or almost black before you can use them, store them in the freezer. The peel acts as a protective cover for the frozen flesh.

ROASTED OVERRIPE BANANA SPLITS

2 overripe bananas (the peels should be black)

1½ teaspoons unsalted butter

1 tablespoon brown sugar

¼ cup rum

Salt

1 to 2 scoops Coffee Grounds Ice Cream (page 221), or other ice cream, not too sweet

¼ cup Banana–Coffee Grounds Bread Crumbs (at right)

Preheat the oven to 350°F.

Make a lengthwise slit in the peel of each banana and wrap in foil. On a baking sheet, roast the bananas in their skins for 10 minutes, until soft and cooked. Remove from the oven and let rest on the baking sheet until the bananas are cool enough to handle. Open the foil, pouring off the liquid into a dish to reserve for drizzling later. Scrape the banana pulp out of the skin into a bowl. Store the peels in the freezer for serving.

In a medium pan over medium heat, melt the butter and add the banana pulp, brown sugar, and rum. Cook, stirring for about 7 minutes, until it thickens and little brown bits begin to collect on the bottom of the pan. Add a pinch of salt.

When ready to serve, stuff the peels with the banana filling and serve with a scoop of ice cream. Finish with coffee bread crumbs and a drizzle of the reserved banana syrup.

SERVES 2 / TIME: 20 MIN

OVERRIPE BANANA–COFFEE GROUNDS BREAD

This simple recipe brings together the hyper-concentrated flavors and wonderful moisture of overripe bananas and coffee grounds. It can be mixed by hand, but if you do use an electric mixer, do not overmix.

½ cup (1 stick) unsalted butter, softened

1 cup sugar

2 eggs

1½ cups mashed, very ripe bananas (3 large or 4 medium)

1 tablespoon used coffee grounds

1¾ cups all-purpose flour

1 teaspoon baking soda

½ teaspoon baking powder

½ teaspoon kosher salt

Preheat the oven to 350°F. Grease a 9 × 5 × 3-inch loaf pan.

Cream the butter and sugar together in a large bowl. Add the eggs, mashed bananas, and coffee grounds until blended.

In a medium bowl, combine the flour, baking soda, baking powder, and salt. Add the dry ingredients to the banana mixture and mix until just combined.

Pour the batter into the loaf pan. Bake for 30 minutes, until the loaf has risen and cracks in the center.

Let cool on a wire rack. Turn upside down to serve.

MAKES 1 LOAF /
ACTIVE TIME: 45 MIN /
INACTIVE TIME: 30 MIN

BANANA–COFFEE GROUNDS BREAD CRUMBS

After enjoying your bread, bake and dry the leftover crumbs for a crunchy crumble topping, wonderful on ice cream or in granola. Whatever amount of crumbs you have, you can use.

1 cup (or more) crumbs from Overripe Banana–Coffee Grounds Bread (at left)

Preheat the oven to 300°F.

Spread the banana bread crumbs in a single layer on a parchment-covered baking sheet. Toast on an upper rack in the oven for 30 minutes, until dry and crisp.

Store in an airtight container for up to 7 days.

TIME: 30 MIN

SPROUT SALAD WITH BANANA PEEL MISO

Here, banana and miso provide salty and sweet flavors—without the addition of any sugar or salt—for a delicious and filling lunch.

1 banana peel, diced, plus three slices mashed flesh (about 1 inch of banana)
1 teaspoon neutral oil
1 tablespoon red miso
1 cup mixed sprouts (pea, lentil, and kidney bean sprouts), available at health food stores or DIY, see box at right

In a medium pan, sauté the banana peel in the oil over medium heat until soft, about 30 seconds, stirring constantly so the pieces do not burn. Add the banana flesh and mash it into the peel mixture. Remove from heat and mix in the miso.

In a medium pot, cover the sprout mixture with 1 cup water and bring to a boil. Cook for 1 minute, until slightly softened but still firm. Drain.

Serve in bowls, mixing about 2 tablespoons banana miso with 4 to 5 tablespoons sprouts for each serving.

SERVES 2 / TIME: 20 MIN

BEAN SPROUTS: DO TRY THIS AT HOME

BEAN SPROUTS provide delicious nutty flavor, crunch, and nutrients to sandwiches, salads, and stir-fried dishes. It's easy to make them at home, using old beans in your pantry.

In a glass bowl or mason jar, cover 1 cup of lentils or peas (not split peas and not kidney beans) with water and let sit overnight. The next day, strain out the water and cover the bowl or jar to protect it from debris but still allow air flow; cheesecloth or a fine mesh strainer will work. Once a day for the next two days rinse the sprouts in water and put them back in the bowl. After 3 days they should be sprouting well and can be kept chilled in the refrigerator up to a week.

Other Ways to Enjoy Bananas

CARAMELIZED OVERRIPE BANANAS:

Make this simple Chinese dessert by slicing the bananas ½ inch thick, then sprinkle with sugar and fry in a pan with butter on both sides to caramelize.

BANANA HALVA (INDIAN DESSERT) WITH PISTACHIOS:

Mash 5 very overripe bananas, and fry in a skillet with oil over high heat for about 5 minutes, turn down the heat and cook until it forms a toffee coating, about another 10 minutes. Sprinkle with a teaspoon of sugar and stir in ¼ cup chopped pistachios. As it begins to cool, cut into squares. Serve at room temperature.

BANANA SMOOTHIE:

Combine an overripe banana with 1 cup yogurt. Add a cup of frozen berries and blend until smooth.

CHEWY BANANA CHIPS

Unlike store-bought banana chips that are fried to a crisp in oil and sugar, these banana chips amplify the flavor of the raw fruit for a slightly sweet and chewy treat.

2 overripe bananas, peeled and chopped

Prepare a dehydrator or preheat the oven to 150°F. Line a baking sheet with parchment paper.

Combine the bananas and 2 tablespoons water in a blender and puree.

Spread in a thin layer on the baking sheet and dehydrate at 150°F for 6 hours, or until chewy. Cut into chip-size pieces or tear into strips. Either way they will disappear quickly.

MAKES APPROXIMATELY 1 CUP / ACTIVE TIME: 15 MIN / TOTAL TIME: 6 HRS

TMW

OVERRIPE BLUEBERRY BANANA PANCAKES

The beauty of cooking pancakes at home is that you can pack them with so much fruit that the result is more like cooked fruit with a little bit of pancake. Of course, you can also lighten up on the quantities of fruit called for in the recipe.

1 cup whole-grain pancake mix, plus ingredients to make standard pancakes
2 overripe bananas, peeled and sliced
Some overripe blueberries (if you have them)
About 1 tablespoon unsalted butter or oil

Follow the instructions on the pancake package to make the pancake batter. Stir in the banana slices and blueberries (if using).

Heat a skillet over medium heat. Lightly grease with oil or butter. Gently ladle in the batter to form 4 pancakes, making sure that the fruit is evenly distributed. Cook for about 2 minutes, until little bubbles appear on the tops and the undersides are golden brown. Flip the pancakes and cook for another minute, until done to your taste. Repeat, adding more butter or oil if the pan is dry, until the batter is finished.

TIME: 20 MINUTES

BERRIES

BERRIES ARE AN IMPORTANT part of summer life in Denmark. During the long, sunny days everyone goes outdoors to pick wild strawberries, bilberries, blueberries, currants, and gooseberries. When I came to North America I found delicious wild varieties here, too: wineberries, blueberries, huckleberries, and elderberries, plus, of course, a bounty of cultivated blueberries, raspberries, blackberries, and strawberries.

I enjoy these jewels unripe, ripe, and overripe, and I use them in both sweet and savory dishes. Because they become mushy and wrinkled, quickly drying, freezing, fermenting, and preserving them are a large part of enjoying them.

WRINKLED BERRY SALSA WITH HERB & KALE STEMS

Berries bring sweetness to an otherwise savory salsa.

2 cups (1-inch) chopped kale stems (or other ribs of any leafy vegetable tops, such as chard, collards, or beets)

4 tablespoons olive oil

Kosher salt

1 cup wrinkled imperfect blueberries

1 cup finely chopped scraps (stems and leaves) of fresh herbs (parsley, cilantro, mint, rosemary, dill, tarragon)

1 clove garlic, finely minced

Grated zest of 1 lemon

2 tablespoons fresh lemon juice

¼ cup chopped Pickled Rose Petals (page 265) or other lightly pickled condiment

Freshly ground black pepper, to taste

Day-Old Charred Garlic Bread (page 154)

Brush the kale stems with 1 tablespoon of the oil and sprinkle with ¼ teaspoon salt. Heat a dry cast iron skillet over high heat. Add the kale stems and sear for 5 minutes, until lightly browned and softened.

In a medium bowl, combine the seared ribs with the remaining 3 tablespoons olive oil, the blueberries, herb stems, garlic, lemon zest, lemon juice, and pickled rose petals. Add salt and pepper to taste. Serve on top the garlic bread.

SERVES 4 / TIME: 30 MIN

OVERRIPE BERRY VINEGAR

The sweetness of late-season, very ripe fruit works well in vinegar and can be enjoyed for months. It's so simple to make it yourself and fresher than store-bought berry vinegar. I used berries but have also experimented with cherries, oranges, and other fruits. Resist any urge to throw out the vinegared berries in the jars. Serve them with ice cream or the sweet Overripe Berry Parfait (page 113).

1 cup very ripe but not moldy berries (raspberries and blueberries but also cranberries, crabapples, even orange peels)
1 cup white wine vinegar

In a medium pot, cover the berries with the vinegar and lightly mash to a pulp with a fork. Heat over low heat for 1 minute.

Remove from the heat and pour into a sterilized jar. Cool, then store for up to a week in the refrigerator.

MAKES 1 QUART / TIME: 15 MIN

OVERRIPE BERRY PARFAIT

This is a sweet European-style parfait with vinegared berries. I like it aerated, using a vacuum lock box, but the recipe below works well at home. Sometimes I add a layer of pralines on the bottom.

1 cup wrinkled or very ripe berries
½ cup plus 2 tablespoons water
½ cup sugar
4 eggs
2 cups heavy cream

Crush the berries in a small pot and add ½ cup water. Bring to a boil. Reduce the heat and simmer until the berries are thick and syrupy, about 15 minutes, depending on how ripe and juicy they are.

In a small saucepan, bring the sugar and the remaining 2 tablespoons water to a boil and cook until the temperature reaches 244°F.

In a mixer with a whisk attachment, beat the eggs and pour in the sugar syrup. Add the berry syrup. Continue to mix for 10 minutes, until the mixture has become thick and ribbon-like.

In a large bowl, whip the cream until stiff peaks form. Transfer the berry mixture to a large bowl and fold in the whipped cream. Spoon into a shallow pan and freeze overnight or up to 24 hours, until firm.

SERVES 10-12 / ACTIVE TIME: 30 MIN /
INACTIVE TIME: OVERNIGHT

TMW

OVERRIPE BERRY SHRUB

A shrub is an old way to use fruits that are becoming overripe. Shrubs—flavored waters—fell out of favor with the advent of refrigeration, but there is renewed interest now, because they are not too sweet and are a great fruity flavor base for innovative sodas and cocktails. Or enjoy them alone by splashing over ice in a glass and adding water to dilute to suit your taste. The flavor enhancement should be more tangy than sweet.

2 cups overripe (but not rotten or moldy) berries
1 cup sugar
1 cup cider vinegar

In a medium pot, mix the berries with the sugar. Bring to a boil, reduce the heat, and simmer for 15 minutes. Add the cider vinegar and continue to simmer for another 15 minutes. Refrigerate in a mason jar.

MAKES APPROXIMATELY 2 CUPS / TIME: 30 MINUTES

Other Ways to Enjoy Overripe Berries

FREEZE on a baking tray and then store in sealed freezer bags for use later in smoothies or baking.

DEHYDRATE (see Nature's Candy, page 114) and use to make fruit roll-ups.

FOLD into baked goods.

PUREE for sauces, syrups, or coulis.

NATURE'S
CANDY:
DEHYDRATED FRUIT

OLDER FRUIT can be dehydrated to concentrate the flavor. No one will care if it looked ugly or wrinkled before it was dried. Dry fruit in a dehydrator or oven at 125° to 135°F, until dense and still slightly chewy. The timing is going to depend on what type of fruit you are drying as well as the condition, water content, and relative humidity. Also, the more surface area that is available for drying, the quicker the fruit will dry. Do not turn up the heat to quicken the drying time as it can cause case hardening on the outside, which will prevent drying on the inside.

CITRUS

THE USES FOR CITRUS FRUITS in cooking are as endless as the world is vast. And not just the flesh and juices, the peels and the leaves from their trees are fair game as well. Italians use lemon tree leaves to wrap up cheese and meat and fish for grilling to keep the juices in as well as impart a lemony flavor to the food. In Morocco, preserved lemons are essential for every kitchen. In Southeast Asia, the leaves of local lime trees are used extensively—chopped, stir-fried, and stuffed in sausage. In China, dried orange peels are prized in tea and in savory dishes, such as dried tangerine peels in shredded beef.

USED GRAPEFRUIT GIN & TONIC

The sweet tang of grapefruit syrup replaces the tonic for a refreshing and natural twist on the classic G&T. I developed this and all the other cocktail recipes in this book with Michael Reynolds, co-owner of the downtown New York City bar Black Crescent (and formerly of the iconic Booker and Dax cocktail bar). You can find several other unique cocktails that we developed together on the following pages.

2 ounces (¼ cup) gin
¾ ounce (1½ tablespoons) Used Grapefruit Syrup
    (at right)
½ ounce (1 tablespoon) lime juice
¼ ounce (½ tablespoon) simple syrup (1 part sugar
    dissolved in 1 part water)
Ice
½ ounce (1 tablespoon) soda water

In a shaker, combine the gin, grapefruit syrup, lime juice, and simple syrup. Fill the shaker with ice and shake vigorously until the contents are completely chilled. Pour the liquid through a fine-mesh strainer into a coupe glass. Top off with the soda water.

MAKES 1 COCKTAIL / TIME: 5 MIN

USED GRAPEFRUIT SYRUP

Most people eat a grapefruit by cutting out each pink fleshy segment with a knife. Left behind for the garbage are the peels, the membranes, even a fair amount of flesh, and the juice. Save them all for this syrup, which can also be made into a vinaigrette for salads or vegetables.

Flesh scraped from 2 leftover organic large
    grapefruit halves
2 grapefruit peels (1 inch square each)
½ cup grapefruit juice, squeezed from the halves
1 cup sugar
½ cup water

In a medium saucepan, combine the grapefruit flesh, peels, and juice with the sugar and water. Bring to a boil, then turn down the heat to low. Simmer for 5 minutes until the syrup starts turning slightly brown and is reduced to about 1 cup.

Remove from the heat, let cool, and strain. Compost the solids and store the syrup in the refrigerator for up to 15 days.

**MAKES ABOUT ONE CUP, enough for 15 cocktails /
TIME: 20 MIN**

Other Ways to Enjoy Citrus Scraps and Rinds

MAKE CITRUS-INFUSED WATER:

Throw 2 lemon, lime, orange, or grapefruit halves (or any combination thereof) in a gallon container of water in the refrigerator. It lasts for weeks. Add some mint.

TIP: Peel the rinds before juicing lemons. You will be less likely to throw them out since it's much easier to peel before the lemon has been cut and squeezed.

MAKE DRIED FLAVORINGS:

Dry the peels whole or zest them to flavor tea, rice, and other dishes.

MAKE CITRUS SALT:

Mix lemon zest with thyme or other herbs and store in a glass jar with salt for a delicious seasoning.

MAKE PRESERVED LEMONS:

In a mason jar, combine 8 leftover lemon halves, ¼ cup salt, and ¼ cup sugar. Add the juice of 1 lemon. Shake and store for several weeks in a mason jar in the refrigerator. When ready to use, rinse the salt off the rind and chop or slice. Use in salads and stews.

T M W

CANDIED CITRUS PEELS

1½ cups organic orange and lemon peels, trimmed of excess white pith
¾ cup sugar
½ cup water

Cut the peels to about 3-inch lengths. Blanch them in a medium pot of boiling water until tender, about 10 minutes. Set on a wire rack to drain.

In a medium pot, make a simple syrup by combining ½ cup of the sugar and the water over medium heat until the sugar dissolves. Add the peels and cook over low heat for another 10 minutes. Dry the peels on the wire rack for about 1 hour. (Use the leftover syrup in cocktails or drinks.)

Once the peels are stiff and somewhat sticky, roll them in the remaining ¼ cup sugar until coated. Store in a cool, dry, sealed container for up to a month.

MAKES 1 ½ CUPS / ACTIVE TIME: 25 MINUTES /
INACTIVE TIME: 1 HOUR

HOW TO MAKE
FRUIT LIQUEUR

WASH AND CLEAN the imperfect or soft (but not rotten) fruit. Place in a ½-gallon mason jar and pour enough alcohol (vodka, brandy, gin, or rum) to cover. Put a cover on the jar. Let steep for 3 to 5 days. If you are going to use the liqueur within a couple of days, you can leave the fruit in, but if you want to keep it longer, strain out the fruit. The strained liqueur will be good for years.

LEMONADE
IS ONLY THE
HALF OF IT

THIS BOOK uses a lot of fresh lemons, so you may end up with leftover lemon halves and rinds. Don't throw them out. The lemon skin contains most of the essential flavorful oils.

When using the rinds, choose organic lemons, as citrus skin absorbs pesticides. And go for thin-skinned varieties with less of the white pith, since it tends to be bitter and has to be scraped away.

I like to dry citrus peels on the radiator in my apartment to make tea. But sometimes before I can, my girlfriend Kelly snags them for her homemade body scrub. Here's her simple recipe:

KELLY'S BODY SCRUB

Pulp from 6 carrots, dried for 1 to 2 days
    on the radiator and ground into a powder
    in a coffee grinder
Peel from 1 orange, dried for 1 to 2 days
    on the radiator and ground into a powder
    in a coffee grinder
1 tablespoon used coffee grounds
2 tablespoons coconut oil

Mix together in a bowl and keep in a 1-cup lidded container.

CUCUMBER

ALTHOUGH IT IS ALMOST always treated as a vegetable, the cucumber is technically a fruit—a botanical berry, to be precise. Like its cousins the squashes and gourds, the cucumber grows from a vine. Although we have yet to see them in any grocery store, the cucumber's stems, tips, young leaves, and flowers are also edible. Because they have such a high water content (more than 90 percent in some varieties), cucumbers don't store very well. They can dry up, wrinkle, and lose their crispness quickly. Here's what you can do with them.

CHARRED WRINKLED CUCUMBERS

Cucumbers don't have to only be eaten raw. I like to cook them on a grill, or over the flame of a gas stove. The important thing is that one side is charred (or lightly burned), and the other is raw. Serve on the side with grilled fish or meats.

2 unpeeled cucumbers (more or less; wrinkled is fine), cut in half lengthwise

Over a hot fire (about 400°F) roast/char the cucumber halves on the peel side until the peel is browned. Leave the open flesh side raw.

Alternate method: Set the oven to broil, place the cucumbers, peel side up, on a baking sheet, on the top rack. Broil, watching the charring closely; as soon as the cucumber wrinkles and browns, remove from the oven. Let cool.

SERVES 4 / TIME: 15 MIN

BRINED CUCUMBER PEEL

I love a great pickle for banh mi sandwiches, burgers, reubens, or as a condiment. Use unwaxed organic cucumbers to avoid potential pesticide residue.

Peels from 3 (or more! What is in your refrigerator?) unwaxed organic cucumbers
4 cups water
0.7 ounces (3½ teaspoons) kosher salt (exact proportion is critical for brining)

Pack the cucumber peels into a sterilized large ceramic pot or gallon mason jar (not metal).

Pour the water into the container and add the salt. Put with a lid that fits inside the crock (a drop lid) on the solution and a weight so that the peels do not rise above the salt solution.

Leave the container covered at room temperature for 3 to 5 days, checking it from time to time, until it starts to bubble. If a white bubbly foam appears, skim it off. If a dark scum or mold appears, this means that the jar or some other element was not sterile and you will need to throw it out in the compost.

Taste for sourness and if it is sour enough, lightly rinse the cucumbers, transfer to a jar, and refrigerate for up to 3 weeks.

MAKES 1½ CUPS OR MORE / ACTIVE TIME: 10 MIN / TOTAL TIME: 3 TO 5 DAYS

Other Ways to Enjoy Wrinkled Cucumbers and Cucumber Scraps

STIR-FRY CHILI CUCUMBERS:
Peel and cut a (wrinkly or not) cucumber in half and slice into ½-inch-wide half-moons. Stir-fry with chili bean paste and sesame oil for a quick weekday side dish.

BRINE THE "BUTTS":
Brine the ends of the cucumber (or butts, as they are referred to in the pickle industry). Traditionally they have been discarded, but recently enterprising chefs are intentionally buying these perfectly good parts to make pickles.

PEARS

THE PEAR, THE FRUIT of the pear tree, shares the genus *Prunus* with cherries, plums, and peaches. The seeds, leaves, and bark of the tree contain some amounts of hydrogen cyanide, which can be toxic in certain dosages. On the other hand, the pear flesh, skin, and juice are simply divine. When a pear becomes overripe, its natural sweetness is more addictive than one-dimensional sugar. Besides its obvious applications in desserts, it can be wonderful in savory meat and fish dishes.

PORK RIBS WITH OVERRIPE-PEAR BARBECUE SAUCE

On my days off, when I visit friends and the weather is fine, they usually want to grill outdoors. Everyone has their own way of cooking their ribs. I like to make them meltingly soft, brining them first by rubbing them with salt and refrigerating overnight, then basting them with my sweet and tangy overripe-pear sauce. To finish the flavor, I garnish the ribs with a raw citrusy green, like sorrel stems or spruce tips (see page 249), depending on the season.

2 pounds mushy overripe pears (see Note), stems and seeds discarded (peels still on), grated 4 cups
½ cup plus 1 tablespoon Kosher salt
1 full slab pork ribs (3–4 individual ribs per person)
2 cups apple cider vinegar
Chopped sorrel or spruce tips (or other citrusy herb), for garnish

To make the pear juice for the sauce, in a medium crock or plastic container, mix the grated pears with 1 tablespoon of the salt and cover with a lid that fits inside the crock (a drop lid). Place a weight on top of the lid and leave at room temperature. (If you don't have a crock with a weighted lid, you can use a large cabbage leaf to cover the fruit and put a mason jar filled with water on top.) Let sit overnight. (For a more fermented liquid, add some whey and let the pears ferment for up to a week, checking every few days to skim off any foam on the top.)

The next day the salt should have caused the fruit to give up more liquid. Strain, reserving both the juice and the grated pulp. You should have about 1½ cups juice and 2 cups pulp.

For the ribs: Rub the ribs with ½ cup salt and refrigerate overnight.

The next day, preheat the oven to 275°F. Brush any excess salt and liquid from the ribs. Place the ribs in a roasting pan with enough water to cover. Bake for about 1½ hours until the meat is nearly falling off the bone. You can prep these ribs ahead of time until ready to serve.

Meanwhile, make the sauce: In a small pan over low heat, combine the pear juice and vinegar and reduce the juice to a thin syrup, about 30 minutes.

Add the grated pear pulp, turn up the heat to medium, and cook until thickened, about 12 minutes. Remove from the heat.

To serve: Preheat the oven to 375°F. Line a baking sheet with parchment paper.

Cut the ribs apart, between the bones, and place on the baking sheet. Brush liberally with about half of the sauce. Roast for about 6 minutes, until a caramelized crust has developed. Place the ribs on a platter and sprinkle liberally with chopped sorrel stems and/or spruce tips. Serve with the remaining sauce.

NOTE:
Since this recipe is about using scraps, if you don't have enough pears, mix in another fruit (perhaps apples or plums) to make 2 pounds.

SERVES 4 / ACTIVE TIME: 45 MIN / TOTAL TIME: 1 DAY or longer

PUMPKIN

IN OCTOBER THERE ARE so many pumpkins for sale for carving and decoration. (In fact, every year Americans buy about 1.1 billion pounds of pumpkins, according to the National Agricultural Statistics Service.) Seeing all this American plenty got me energized to cook them. Whole pumpkins come in so many different shapes, sizes, and colors, so rather than developing a one-size-fits-all recipe, I came up with two different cooking methods, based on size. We are not going to mislead you into thinking there is a secret equation that x pounds of pumpkin equals x cups of puree. Larger pumpkins can have less puree if they are hollow. Some small pumpkin varieties have more flesh.

BOILED LARGE PUMPKIN

A large Halloween pumpkin, intended for carving, usually has only 2 inches of flesh. Still, it yields a great deal of goodness. For instance, an 8-pound (2-foot-diameter) pumpkin can produce enough puree for three pies, plus seeds, which can be caramelized for a decadent snack. But cooking it can present challenges. It can be difficult to cut up such a large fibrous fruit, and it's tricky to fit it in a small oven. So I recommend the following approach.

1 large pumpkin—anything bigger than a foot and weighing more than 7 pounds

With a heavy cleaver, cut off the bottom of the pumpkin; reserve for Layered Pumpkin Pie (page 129). Chop the rest of the pumpkin into 5-inch pieces. Scoop out the seeds and set aside to roast later (page 129).

In a large pot over high heat, combine the pumpkin chunks and 5 cups water. Bring to a boil, reduce the heat, and simmer for 45 minutes, until softened. Drain. In batches, puree the chunks in a food processor until coarsely smooth, about 3 minutes. Refrigerate for a few days in a closed container or measure and freeze in batches for up to 6 months.

ACTIVE TIME: 30 MIN / INACTIVE TIME: 45 MIN

ROASTED SMALL OR MEDIUM PUMPKIN

1 small to medium pumpkin—anything under 7 pounds and less than a foot across (vertically or horizontally)

Preheat the oven to 350°F.

Cut slits in the top of the pumpkin for ventilation. Place on a baking sheet and roast for 1½ to 2 hours, until the top sags down. Don't worry about overcooking a bit. Let cool.

Scoop out the seeds and pulp and set aside. When scooping, reserve the skin as well as the thin layer of flesh next to the skin for Pumpkin Skin Powder (page 127).

When thoroughly cooked, puree in a food processor until coarsely smooth. Refrigerate in a closed container for a few days or freeze for up to six months.

MAKES 1–4 CUPS PUREE / ACTIVE TIME: 15 MIN / INACTIVE TIME: 1½ TO 2 HRS

PUMPKIN SKIN POWDER

This powder can be used as an additional flavoring or as a flour itself in the crust for the Classic Pumpkin Pie (right) or the Pumpkin Flour Ravioli (page 135). Yield is variable; but a medium pumpkin's skin will yield about ⅓ cup pumpkin skin powder.

Use a dehydrator or preheat the oven to 150°F (or turn down the heat if you just roasted the pumpkin). Scoop out the inside of the small to medium roasted pumpkin, reserving the skin and thin layer of flesh next to the skin. On a baking sheet, place the pumpkin pieces skin side up. Dehydrate for 5–7 hours, until dry and crispy. Grind the pieces in a coffee or spice grinder until powdered. Store in an airtight container for up to 3 months.

ACTIVE TIME: 10 MIN / TOTAL TIME: 5–7 HRS

CLASSIC PUMPKIN PIE

It was fun for me to make an American pumpkin pie— but after I bought some Halloween pumpkins, I heard they are not good for eating. They are perfectly good in a classic pumpkin pie. For a twist I used a little extra pumpkin powder in the crust.

Pumpkin Flour Crust
1 cup all-purpose flour
⅓ cup Pumpkin Skin Powder (left)
Pinch kosher salt
½ cup (1 stick) cold unsalted butter, cubed
1 egg
2 tablespoons cold water

Filling
2 cups fresh pumpkin puree, from a large or smaller (page 125) pumpkin
1 cup cream
½ cup sugar
3 eggs
½ teaspoon kosher salt

For the Crust: Preheat the oven to 350°F.

Combine the crust ingredients in a food processor and pulse until they hold together in a ball. Spritz with a little water if the dough is too dry. On a ¼-inch-thick floured surface, roll out the dough. Fit into a 10-inch tart pan and trim the edges. Chill in the refrigerator for 15 minutes to set.

Line the pie shell crust with parchment paper and fill with pie weights (or dried beans). Bake for 15 minutes. Remove the parchment and pie weights and reduce the heat to 325°F. Bake for another 10 minutes, until the center is light brown. Remove from the oven and let cool.

For the Filling: In a large bowl, combine the filling ingredients until smooth. Pour the mixture into the pie shell. Bake at 325°F for 1 hour, until the filling has set (a little jiggly but not wet). Cool on a rack.

MAKES 1 (10-INCH) PIE / ACTIVE TIME: 45 MIN / INACTIVE TIME: 1 HR

LAYERED PUMPKIN PIE

This recipe began as an experiment and turned out great. It uses the bottom of the pumpkin as a natural crust. Then again, maybe it's not as new as I think: I have heard that European settlers made the first pumpkin pie from a whole pumpkin by scooping out the seeds and filling the inside with honey and milk and then baking it in hot ashes.

1 pumpkin bottom, cut from a medium to large pumpkin into a shallow (2-inch-deep) bowl

3 tablespoons sugar

1 cup Caramelized Roasted Pumpkin Seeds (at right)

2 cups pumpkin puree, from a large or smaller (page 125) pumpkin

1 cup cream

½ cup sugar

3 eggs

½ teaspoon kosher salt

Anywhere from 5–50 strands of Pumpkin Jerky (page 133), optional

Preheat the oven to 350°F.

Sprinkle the fleshy side of the pumpkin bowl liberally with the sugar. Place the bowl face down (skin side up) on a baking sheet and roast for 20 minutes. Flip it to skin side down and roast for another 10 minutes, until the top has caramelized and the shell is cooked. Sprinkle the pumpkin seeds inside the bowl.

In a large bowl, combine the pumpkin puree, cream, sugar, eggs, and salt. Pour the filling inside the pumpkin bowl.

Reduce the oven temperature to 325°F. Bake the pie for 1 hour or more, until the filling has set (a little jiggly but not wet). Cool on a rack. Top with the pumpkin jerky and serve.

**MAKES 1 PIE / ACTIVE TIME: 30 MIN /
INACTIVE TIME: 1 HR or more**

CARAMELIZED ROASTED PUMPKIN SEEDS

The caramelization makes these an addictive snack as well as a crunchy addition to soups, frostings, and salads. See the Layered Pumpkin Pie at left or Pumpkin-Seed Rye Crackers on page 131.

2 cups sugar

2 cups water

2 cups pumpkin seeds (requires a 3-pound or larger pumpkin)

Preheat the oven to 325°F.

Rinse the seeds in hot water to remove the pulp.

In a medium pot, combine the sugar and water and bring to a simmer. Add the seeds and simmer until they are soft and sweetened, about 15 minutes. Drain.

Spread the seeds in a single layer on a baking sheet. Toast in the oven until crispy, about 15 minutes. Mix and toast for another 15 minutes, until uniformly lightly browned. Let cool so the sugar will harden.

Store in an airtight container for up to 15 days. When ready to use, smash the seeds, if you like, so that they break into crumbles.

MAKES ABOUT 2 CUPS / TIME: 45 MIN

PUMPKIN-SEED RYE CRACKERS

These crispy and dry crackers are equally good cut into square crackers or as larger 6–8-inch crispbreads as in the photo. Crispbread, or *knaekbrod*, is a staple for many Nordic people and has long been thought of as poor man's food.

1 cup **Caramelized Pumpkin Seeds (page 129)**
2 cups **all-purpose flour**
1 cup **rye flour**
¾ cup **cold water**
2 tablespoons **nut or seed oil**
1 **egg**
Kosher salt
½ cup or more **mixed seeds (pumpkin and others)**
½ cup **chopped fresh herbs (e.g., thyme or oregano)**

Place ¾ cup of the pumpkin seeds in a blender or spice grinder and pulse until evenly ground into a powder.

In a food processor, combine the pumpkin seed powder with the flours, water, oil, egg, and 1 teaspoon salt and pulse until it forms a firm, nonstick ball. Adjust with more flour if sticky. Cut the dough into 4 equal portions. Wrap in plastic wrap and chill for 30 minutes to relax the dough. You can refrigerate it for up to 3 days if you don't want to make it all at once.

Preheat the oven to 350°F. Line a baking sheet with parchment paper.

When ready to roll, flour the work surface generously. Roll out one portion of dough to a 12 × 8-inch rectangle that is 1/16 to 1/8 inch thick. If the dough becomes sticky, you may need to keep sprinkling the surface with more flour. Cut the dough into 15 squares (roughly 2½ × 2½ inches) or two 6 × 4 crispbreads and transfer to the baking sheet.

With a fork, prick holes over the surface of the dough to prevent the crackers from puffing up during baking. Spritz the surface with water to enable the seeds to stick to the dough. Sprinkle with one-fourth of the seeds and herbs, and a bit more salt.

Bake for 20 minutes, rotating the baking sheet halfway through, until the crackers are golden brown, dry, and brittle. Remove from the oven and let cool for 10 minutes. Break the crackers into the desired size.

Repeat with the remaining dough to make 3 more batches. You can do multiple sheets at the same time, or even refrigerate and finish up later.

The baked crackers keep well in a sealed container in the pantry for a month in low humidity.

**MAKES 60 CRACKERS or 7 crispbreads /
TIME: 1 HR 10 MIN**

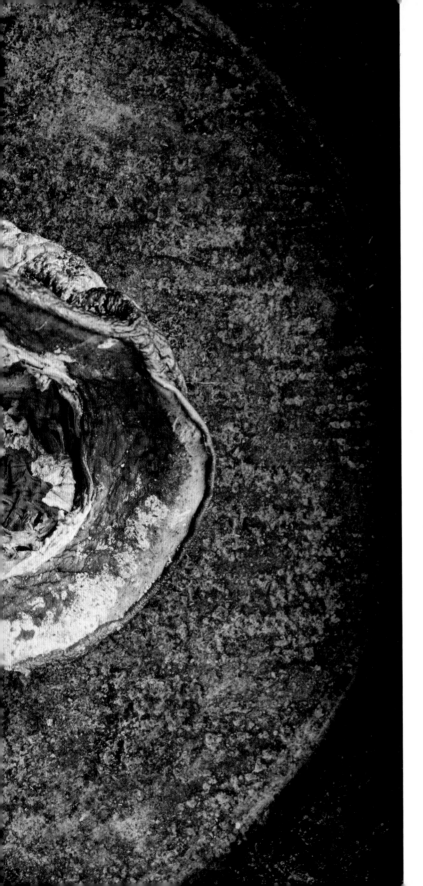

PUMPKIN JERKY

Enjoy this chewy and intensely flavored jerky as a snack or use to finish dishes with beautiful color and pumpkin flavor. You'll need half of a pumpkin: Use a cleaver to cut a medium pumpkin crosswise in half. (Roast the other half for puree, page 125, and/or powder, page 127, and caramelize the seeds, page 129.) Yield will depend on the size and meatiness of the pumpkin.

3 tablespoons kosher salt
½ medium (2-pound or 7-inch)
pumpkin, scraped of seeds

Set the dehydrator at 150°F.

Spread the salt with your hands evenly around the inner (flesh) side of the pumpkin half.

Dehydrate the pumpkin half at 150°F for 5 to 7 days, until the flesh feels like a shriveled apricot and is chewy rather than crisp. It may take longer depending on the size of the pumpkin. You can shorten the drying time by cutting the pumpkin into large steak-size slices to create more surface area. (The pumpkin may collect some water in the bottom while dehydrating as a result of the salting. If so, pour out this liquid.)

When the pumpkin jerky is ready, slice or pull it into shreds. Store in an airtight container for up to two weeks.

ACTIVE TIME: 15 MIN /
TOTAL TIME: 5 TO 7 DAYS or more

PUMPKIN FLOUR RAVIOLI WITH SHAVED RAW CHESTNUTS & ROASTED PUMPKIN SEEDS

The pumpkin powder in the flour gives the ravioli a beautiful autumnal color.

Pumpkin Filling

1½ cups pumpkin flesh cut into chunks

¼ cup chopped shallots

1 clove garlic, minced

2 tablespoons olive oil

1 egg

1 cup ricotta cheese

Kosher salt and freshly ground black pepper, to taste

Ravioli Dough

1 cup all-purpose flour

1½ tablespoons Pumpkin Skin Powder (page 127)

1 egg plus 1 egg yolk

1 tablespoon olive oil

¼ teaspoon kosher salt

For Serving

1 cup grated Parmesan cheese

1–3 tablespoons Caramelized Roasted Pumpkin Seeds (page 129)

2 raw chestnuts, peeled and sliced thinly, if in season (optional)

For the filling: Preheat the oven to 350°F. In a medium bowl, toss the pumpkin with the shallots, garlic, and olive oil and spread out in a single layer on a baking sheet. Bake for 35 minutes, until tender. Let cool slightly.

Puree in a blender. Transfer to a large bowl and add the egg, ricotta, and salt and pepper and combine well. The filling can be made ahead of time and refrigerated for up to 3 days.

For the ravioli: In a large bowl, mix the flour, pumpkin powder, egg and egg yolk, olive oil, and salt. Transfer to a floured work surface and knead for 4 to 5 minutes; the dough should feel firm and smooth. Divide the dough in half, wrap in plastic, and chill in the refrigerator for at least 30 minutes, preferably overnight.

Roll out each piece of dough into very thin 8 × 11-inch sheets. Drop about ½ teaspoonfuls of the filling in rows an inch apart onto one dough sheet. Place the other sheet on top and press lightly with your fingers around each spoonful of filling. Using a ravioli cutter, cut out each ravioli in a pillow shape. The raviolis can be refrigerated for up to 1 day or frozen on a baking sheet, transferred to a freezer bag, and frozen for up to 2 weeks.

To serve: Bring a large pot of salted water to a boil. Add the ravioli and cook for 3 to 5 minutes, until slightly translucent. Drain and toss while still hot with the Parmesan, pumpkin seeds, and sliced chestnuts.

SERVES 2 / TIME: 2 HRS

TOMATOES

THE TOMATO IS THE berry-like fruit of the tomato vine or bush. Tomatoes must be stored at room temperature (not in the refrigerator) in order to retain their flavor. Unpackaged tomatoes become overripe and mushy in a matter of days, making them no longer prime for slicing raw. But this juiciness and flavor can be preserved for wonderful effect.

Parts of the tomato fruit, other than the flesh, are not only perfectly fine to eat, but highly nutritious. The skins have significantly higher levels of phenolics, flavonoids, ascorbic acid, and antioxidants compared to the pulp. Some studies have found that as much as 30 percent of the weight of the tomato is wasted when the skin, core, and seeds are removed for processing tomatoes into paste.

TOMATO BROTH (DASHI)

This light dashi extracts the flavor of tomatoes and provides a wonderful base to any number of soups. I use it with the Fish Head & Tail Soup (page 181). The flavor can also be concentrated by reducing the broth, then adding vinegar to make a vinaigrette.

2 quarts water
1 (4-ounce) package dried konbu
10 unwanted (i.e., green, ugly, overripe, mushy) tomatoes, moldy parts cut away
½ teaspoon kosher salt

In a large pot, simmer the water and konbu over low heat for 30 minutes, making sure it does not boil. Remove from heat and discard the konbu. Add the tomatoes and simmer over low heat for 2 hours. Strain (save the pulp for Fish Head & Tail Soup, page 181). Season with salt to taste. Refrigerate in a plastic lidded container for up to a month.

MAKES ABOUT 4 CUPS / ACTIVE TIME: 10 MIN / INACTIVE TIME: 2½ HRS

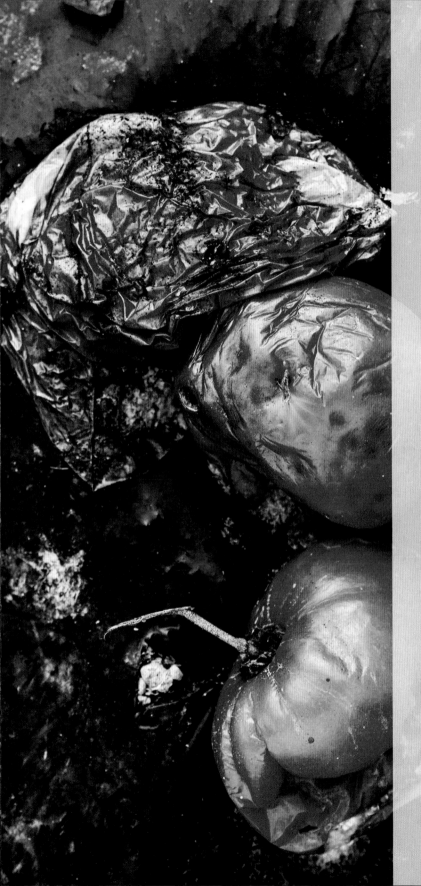

Other Ways to Enjoy Tomato Skins and Seeds

Make mushy (but not slimy or moldy) tomatoes into sauces, pastes, jams, or freeze them for later.

MAKE A COUNTRY-STYLE TOMATO SAUCE:

Trim off any moldy and rotten parts of the tomatoes. In a large stockpot, sauté minced onion and garlic in olive oil until browned. Add tomatoes (including the skins), and herb scraps (thyme, oregano, basil). Reduce heat, cover, and simmer for 2 hours. Cool and puree in a blender. Do not add seasoning until you actually plan to use the sauce, so you can customize it for the dish.

MAKE "SUN-DRIED" TOMATOES IN THE OVEN:

Roma or meaty tomatoes are the best choice here as they have less water. Thinly slice the tomatoes and sprinkle with thyme or oregano stems and a pinch of salt. Spread in a single layer on a parchment-covered baking sheet. Bake in a 250°F oven until slightly dry, chewy but not mushy, about 4 hours. Store in an airtight container or vacuum seal and freeze. In the winter, serve on a toasted English muffin under melted cheese.

WATERMELON

I NOTICE THAT EVERYONE eats watermelons the same way all summer: Cut into half- or quarter-moon slices and then toss the rest. I say: Stand back first and look at the watermelon as a whole. There are so many possibilities. Grill it like a steak, or shave it paper thin and loosely wrap it around some herbs and flowers.

Although we throw them away in the United States, in Chinese culture it's believed that watermelon seeds are a source of good luck. In fact, they are prized even more than the actual watermelon, and are served roasted and salted with the shell on to guests on special occasions. To eat, the shell is cracked to get at the flesh within, which contains antioxidants and other nutritious properties.

GRILLED WATERMELON STEAK WITH OLD HERBS

A thick slice of watermelon can look like a steak. Why not cook it like one? Cut a slab, sprinkle it with herbs, grill it, and carve it like a leg of lamb. (The remaining watermelon flesh can be used for soup, at right, or vinaigrette, page 140.)

1 watermelon or watermelon half

"as you like it" and only if you happen to have them: old aromatic herbs scraps, such as thyme and oregano, including stems

½ cup Watermelon Vinaigrette (page 140) or fruit vinegar (page 97 or 111)

Heat a grill to medium heat.

Cut out a 3-inch-thick round slab from the middle of the watermelon. Scatter with the herb scraps.

Grill the watermelon steak on one side for 2 minutes, until lightly charred. Flip and repeat on the other side. Drizzle with the vinaigrette and carve a slice for each person.

SERVES 4 / TIME: 10 MIN

CHILLED WATERMELON SOUP

This soup is a refreshingly different way to use watermelon bits. I like to spoon it into shallow bowls, about 1 inch deep, add several small chunks of Pickled Watermelon Rind (page 140), top the rind with steamed clams, and finish with herbs, such as passionflower tendrils and wild mint leaves. On its own it makes a refreshing starter to a summer supper, garnished with a few sprigs of herbs.

2 cups chunks of watermelon flesh, preferably grilled for some smoky texture (see Grilled Watermelon Steak, at left)

2 tablespoons sunflower oil or other neutral oil

2 tablespoons cider vinegar

1½ teaspoons kosher salt

Drizzle the watermelon with the oil, vinegar, and salt. Puree in blender for a few seconds until liquid. Strain through a fine-mesh sieve. Cover and refrigerate until chilled.

SERVES 4 / TIME: 10 MIN

Opposite: Chilled Watermelon Soup with pickled watermelon rind, steamed clams, wild mint flower and leaves with passion flower tendrils.

WATERMELON VINAIGRETTE

As with other fruits, a combination of the sweet and sour makes a nice summery vinaigrette over salads or a marinade for fish. It is also a perfect use for "post-barbecue" watermelon that may be slightly mushy or liquidy.

2 cups watermelon flesh chunks, mushy is fine
¾ cup extra virgin olive oil
¼ cup red wine vinegar
Grated zest of 1 lemon
1 teaspoon Dijon mustard
½ teaspoon kosher salt and freshly cracked
**   black pepper, to taste**

Combine the watermelon, olive oil, vinegar, zest, mustard, and salt in a blender and puree until smooth. Season to taste with salt and pepper. Keep in a sealed container in the refrigerator for up to a week.

MAKES 2 CUPS / TIME: 10 MIN

PICKLED WATERMELON RIND

I never had watermelon growing up in Denmark, so now that I'm in the United States, I love having access to them all summer long. The giant rinds are great for pickling. I often preserve them in really big chunks, 6 inches or more, but go ahead and cut them to fit whatever jar you are using. Once ready, I like to cut them into small squares, nestle with raw oysters on shells, and serve on top of ice like oysters on the half shell.

There are two different and basic methods to pickling that I use. The first is the brine. This is what I always used in Denmark: a classic traditional method of preservation. It can sometimes be more temperamental, as there are many factors at play in a brine fermentation, including the condition of the product, its state of ripeness, as well as the humidity and temperature of the location. Some may find it easier to enhance the process by using a commercial starter culture as a catalyst.

I think the brininess of a salt pickle goes exceptionally well with fish and with herbs. The vinegar method of pickling gives you more control in that it does not involve fermentation of the fruit; it is the method I use when I want something quick and easy, a refrigerator pickle.

BRINE-PICKLED WATERMELON RIND

3 ½ tablespoons sea salt (0.7 ounces)

3 cups water

2 pounds (4 cups) cut-up watermelon rinds, peeled of the outermost green layer and any remaining pink flesh

In a gallon jar, combine the salt and water and add the rinds. Place a lid that fits inside the crock (a drop lid) on top of the rinds with a weight on top so that the rinds do not float above the liquid solution. Let pickle until it bubbles and achieves the desired saltiness. The exact time increments are hard to measure. Monitor and test until it is where you want it to be.

Cover and refrigerate for up to a month.

MAKES 4 CUPS / TIME: A FEW DAYS

TMW

VINEGAR-PICKLED WATERMELON RIND (QUICKIE VERSION)

2 pounds (4 cups) cut-up watermelon rinds, which includes the outermost green layer and, importantly, a thin layer of pink flesh

2 cups red wine vinegar

1 cup sugar

¼ cup kosher salt

8 whole cloves

1 teaspoon black peppercorns

1 cup water

Place the rinds in two (1-pint) mason jars or other sealable containers.

In a small saucepan, combine the vinegar, sugar, salt, cloves, and peppercorns. Bring to a boil and cook, stirring continuously, for 2 minutes, until the sugar and salt are dissolved.

Remove from the heat and add the water. Pour this pickling liquid into the jars over the rinds. Let cool with the caps off, cover, and refrigerate. You can start enjoying them the next day, and they will keep for about a month.

MAKES 4 CUPS / TIME: 15 MIN

4

GRAINS

In Denmark grain is
all around, fields and
fields of it.

I LOVE THE EARTHY PURENESS of food made with whole grains. You could fill a paintbox of colors with different grains: millet, rice, buckwheat, rye, barley.

Recently we have lost much of the quality of grains by removing and discarding much of the grain to produce refined flours.

Grains are actually the seeds from the fruit of plants in the grass family. These seeds make up the bulk of food for peoples around the world: not only corn, soy, rice, and wheat, but also the lesser known rye, buckwheat, and oats, which I love, to make bread, pasta, cereals, and baked goods. The grains are usually processed, by rolling, milling, grinding, or other methods, which removes the hull (the outer husk called the bran), the inner seed or germ, and other portions of the fruit. These parts, which are typically discarded or used for animal food and, more recently, biofuel, contain most of the nutrients of the plant. So many "white" flour products have historically had to be enriched and fortified with vitamins; this is why whole grain products are more nutritious and contain more fiber.

Previous spread: Flat Beer & Day-Old-Bread Porridge (page 153) with salted caramel ice cream and apple balsamic vinegar

Left: Ryan Keelan's hands stirring fermenting grain and potatoes.

CORN

IT DIDN'T TAKE ME long after I moved to the United States to see why this indigenous food is considered the taste of American summer and barbecues. And while corn is the largest crop in America, the majority of it is not used as food for people, but rather for animal feed, sweeteners, starch, biofuel, and even toothpaste. The cobs, along with the large leaves, husks, and stalks of the corn plant, are not usually used for food and are referred to as *corn stover*.

I like the shape of corn on the cob, and I like to explore ways to use the entire thing, not just the kernels. So in this section, you'll find recipes that use more than just the kernels and work beautifully together in a delicious flan. The husks wrap the seasoning bundle; the cob cores are charred for the smoky dashi; and the kernels, cooked and raw, star in the flan. I reserve some raw kernels to top the flan for crunchiness, and pair with blueberries for a hint of tanginess and texture.

Corn lasts longer if kept in the husk, but it still should be eaten as soon as possible after purchasing because the sugars that make it sweet start to turn to starch. You can freeze corn kernels on or off the cob by blanching first.

CORN KERNEL FLAN

I like smooth, savory custards because they serve as a good base for flavors and for scraps cooking. In Europe and Mexico, most custards are sweet, but the Japanese custard *chawanmushi* is savory. The name means "steam based tea bowl," meaning for me that it becomes a vessel for potentially anything. I can make different types of base stock "dashi" for the custard as well as include something scrappy and crunchy for texture (grilled cabbage core mini scoops) or…corn.

This savory corn chawanmushi is light and enjoyed best in the summer. It can be kept in the refrigerator and served chilled, or served warm on a rainy or cool day. For a stronger flavored dish, vary the recipe by replacing the corn kernel dashi with Parmesan Rind Broth (page 213) or the initial steps in the Smoky Potato Scrap Broth (page 83).

1⅔ cups raw corn kernels (from about 4 ears of corn) plus ⅓ cup for the topping

4 eggs, at room temperature

1 teaspoon kosher salt

2 cups Charred Corn Cob Dashi (page 149)

12 blueberries, wrinkled ones are fine, halved

Juice of ½ lemon

Mustard oil

In a medium saucepan, cook the kernels in 1 to 2 inches of water for about 8 minutes. Drain, reserving 1½ cups of the cooking liquid. Transfer the liquid and cooked kernels to a food processor and pulse for 15 seconds, until the consistency of a coarse puree. With the back of a wooden spoon, press this puree through a fine mesh sieve to get 1½ cups of corn kernel liquid.

In a large bowl, combine the corn liquid, eggs, and salt, whisking briskly.

Place four 1-cup heatproof bowls in a bamboo steamer. Ladle ½ cup corn-egg mixture into each bowl. Cover and steam over low heat for about 35 minutes, until set. (You could also use a metal steamer, or bake in a 325°F oven.) Remove the bowls from the steamer and cool to room temperature.

Just before serving, pour about ½ cup of warmed corn dashi over each flan, enough to cover. Top each bowl with a few blueberry halves, raw corn kernels, a squeeze of lemon juice, a pinch of salt, and a drizzle of mustard oil (about ¼ teaspoon).

MAKES 4 BOWLS /
TIME: 1 HR, plus time for making the dashi

CHARRED CORN COB DASHI

Dashi is a word I use all the time. I know it is Japanese and not Danish, but it has become an everyday word for chefs in the kitchen. I suppose we started using it whenever we decided to use a seaweed-konbu broth for flavor, rather than stock from fish, chicken, beef, or vegetables. So now I am using the word dashi for all kinds of other flavorful broths, like a base for a sweet or savory custard. Here, charring intensifies the sweet corn flavors and adds a smokiness to the easy vegetarian broth.

4 ears of corn, shucked (save the husks for the husk bundles) and kernels removed (save for Corn Kernel Flan, page 147)
1 (5-inch) piece konbu (cut from a dried sheet; see Resources, page 272)
4 Corn Cob Husk Bundles (at right)
½ teaspoon salt

In a large pot, bring 6 cups of water to a boil.

While the water is heating, grill the corn cobs on an outdoor grill or over the flame of a gas stove, rotating for a few minutes, until each cob is evenly and lightly charred (blistered and black marks appear).

Add the cobs and konbu to the pot and boil, uncovered, for 30 minutes. Turn off the heat, add the corn husk bundles, and steep for at least 45 minutes.

Strain the broth into a large saucepan. Simmer over medium heat until the liquid is reduced by half, about 45 minutes. Add the salt. The corn broth can be frozen or stored in the fridge for up to a month.

MAKES ABOUT 3 CUPS /
ACTIVE TIME: 30 MIN (including making the bundles) /
INACTIVE TIME: 2 HR

CORN COB HUSK BUNDLES

Use corn husks instead of cheesecloth to bundle the herbs and infuse the dashi.

12 corn husks
4 cloves garlic, peeled
8 sprigs fresh parsley
4 small fresh bay leaves
4 (12-inch-long) pieces of butcher's twine

Stack 3 husks and place 1 clove of garlic, 2 sprigs of parsley and a bay leaf in the center. Roll the husks up around the herbs, a making little bouquet garnis and securely tie with twine. Repeat to make 4 bundles.

MAKES 4 BUNDLES / TIME: 15 MIN

Opposite: Corn Kernel Flan with Charred Corn Cob Dashi on top and blueberries and corn kernels

OATS

THE OAT GRAIN IS the seed of a grass that originated as a wild species and may have originally spread as a weed in fields of preferred wheat crops. Oats grow well in cool climates like northwestern Europe and Canada. To process, the oats are hulled (originally through two millstones) and then sifted out to make *groats*, which are a whole grain cereal, chewy and nutritious. You can find groats in health food stores and online if you want to try them (see Resources, page 272).

Most oats are further processed by rolling or steel cutting the hulled oat grains, which are then roasted and packaged for breakfast and for baking and cooking.

LEFTOVER OATMEAL CRISPS

I like to include something crunchy but not too sweet in a dessert. The recipe is very flexible; measurements need not be exact. As long as you have at least 1 cup, it will work. The crisps can be broken up to add crunchiness to ice cream, yogurt, or other smooth pureed sweets, especially Wheat Bran Ice Cream (page 157); it can be used as well as bread crumb–like topping for macaroni and cheese or even with your favorite dip.

1 cup or more leftover cooked oatmeal
Salt
Sweetener, such as brown sugar, molasses, honey

Preheat the oven to 150°F. Line a baking sheet with a Silpat mat or parchment paper.

In a small saucepan, combine the already cooked oatmeal with enough water (¼ to ½ cup) to keep it from sticking to the bottom. Cook over low heat until it is really mushy, about 5 minutes. Add some salt and sweetener.

Spread the oatmeal evenly and thinly on the lined baking sheet and bake for 5 hours, until crisp. Store in an airtight container for a few days.

MAKES A BAKING SHEET OF CRISPS / ACTIVE TIME: 20 MIN / INACTIVE TIME: 5 HRS

RICE

WE DON'T USE A lot of rice in Denmark so I have been amazed at the different kinds of rice that are available here in the United States and the uses for them. I've been inspired by chef Sean Brock's reintroduction of heritage rice in the American South.

Rice is the seed of the rice grass. It is harvested and dried, and the inedible outer layer or husk is removed, along with the bran and germ, to make white rice. (Rice bran can be purchased separately and is a traditional product used for pickling.) For brown rice, only the husk is removed, so it retains the fiber and nutrition that is discarded in making polished white rice.

Rice is the staple food for more than half of the world's population, which leads to a lot of leftovers, and thus numerous uses for day-old (and older) rice.

RICE PORRIDGE

For centuries Asian cuisines have enjoyed some version of rice porridge, usually for breakfast, but also as an easily digestible, comforting meal.

2 cups leftover (day-old or older) cooked rice
6 cups stock (a high-quality chicken stock)
Choice of condiments

Combine the rice and stock in a heavy saucepan and cook over low heat, stirring occasionally, for 1 hour, until creamy like a porridge. (There is room for individual preference in consistency, as some like porridge creamier and some like it more soupy.)

Serve with a variety of condiments, such as leftover chopped meat; minced green onions or chives; something crunchy such as fried shallots; sliced pickled mustards or cabbages; something spicy such as sliced chilies or Sriracha; and dashes of soy sauce, sesame oil, or fish sauce.

SERVES 4 / TIME: 1 HOUR

RICE PUDDING

2 cups leftover (day-old or older) cooked rice
4 cups half-and-half
¼ cup sugar
2 eggs
1 teaspoon vanilla
Loose jam or syrup, for drizzling (optional)

In a medium pot, combine the rice, half-and-half, and sugar and bring to a boil. Reduce the heat and simmer for 25 minutes, until the rice is meltingly soft. Stir often and watch so it does not burn or stick.

Remove from the heat and stir in eggs and vanilla. Spoon into bowls and serve warm or refrigerate. If you like, drizzle with loosened jam or a fruit syrup.

SERVES 6 / TIME: 30 MIN

FRIED RICE

3 tablespoons sesame oil
3 cups leftover (day-old or older) cooked rice
1 teaspoon salt
Choice of refrigerator scraps, such as cooked ham, bacon, or chicken; dark greens; and something crunchy like celery or shredded cabbage
1 tablespoon diced fresh ginger
1 bunch green onions, chopped
1 egg

Heat the oil in a large wok or cast iron skillet over high heat. Add the rice and salt and cook, turning often so it does not stick or burn, until warmed, about 10 minutes. Add the scraps, ginger, and green onions and cook, stirring vigorously, for 3 minutes, until combined and heated. Turn off the heat, add the egg, and stir until incorporated. Serve immediately.

SERVES 4 / TIME: 15 MIN

RYE

RYE IS A MAJOR GRAIN in Northern Europe, where I come from. Thought to have originally grown as a weed in fields of the "luxury" grain (wheat), it is hardy, and therefore a good crop for colder climates. In addition to rye flour, rye berries—which are the whole rye grains from which rye flour is ground—can be purchased in health food stores and online (see Resources, page 272).

FLAT BEER & DAY-OLD-BREAD PORRIDGE

As a child I loved a porridge called *Ollebrod,* made from old rye bread soaked in beer. We ate it for breakfast, but also alongside fish, pork, whatever. It would simmer in a big pot on the stove throughout the day. Guests would come inside and hear it bubbling, grab a spoon, and help themselves. Now, many chefs (Nordic and otherwise) use bread porridge as a canvas for gorgeous flavors, using grains and breads other than just rye.

As a dessert, not a breakfast gruel, porridge becomes a light, delicious, not-too-sweet, and comforting way to conclude a meal. I don't like overly sweet cakes or sugary icing, but ending with something a little naturally sweet and light is satisfying. I love it with a scoop of caramel ice cream and a drizzle of apple balsamic vinegar.

1 pound stale rye (or other) bread, torn into small pieces or crumbled (5½ cups)

2 cups flat beer, preferably dark beer or ale (less than 2 bottles)

1¾ cups sugar, half granulated/half brown

¾ cup heavy cream

⅓ cup dark chocolate chips

Apple balsamic vinegar, for serving

Salted caramel ice cream, for serving

In a medium pot, combine the bread, beer, and sugars over low heat and cook, stirring gently, for about 20 minutes, until the bread is softened and the liquid is absorbed. Add the cream and cook, stirring, for about 10 minutes more, until it starts to thicken. Finally, add the chocolate chips and stir until melted. Remove from the heat and cool. Store in the refrigerator until thoroughly chilled, at least 30 minutes (or up to 2 days).

To serve, spoon into individual bowls, drizzle with apple balsamic vinegar, and add a scoop of caramel ice cream.

SERVES 8 / ACTIVE TIME: 30 MIN / INACTIVE TIME: 30 MIN

WHEAT

WHEAT IS A COMMON GRAIN, but most of us have little idea what it looks like in a field or what parts are discarded through processing it into flour. The wheat kernel heads are cut and then threshed to remove the grain from the rest of the head, which is known as the *chaff*. For white flour, the grain is then milled so that the germ, endosperm, and grain are further separated and discarded or used for feed. These parts of the kernel contain much of the nutrition of the plant. The remaining white grain, ground into flour for bread, pasta and pastries, has to be fortified with vitamins. Whole-wheat flour retains much of the discarded kernel and is a more nutritious choice.

Although wheat flour has a long shelf life, once baked into fresh bread it will only stay soft for one or two days, or up to seven days or more for packaged bread. The package will often have a printed "best by" date that represents when it is softest, after which it may become hard and dry, although it is still perfectly edible. Bread is truly no longer edible when it becomes moldy, at which point it should be composted. Some prepared processed dough rolls and biscuits have oils in them that will go bad; you can tell by the rancid odor. As an ancient staple food, there are many traditional uses for bread once it has passed its peak freshness.

DAY-OLD CHARRED GARLIC BREAD

For a weekend brunch I slather this with the Scraped Salmon Tartare on the Bone (page 169) and serve with Wrinkled Berry Salsa with Herb & Kale Stems (page 108).

18-inch or other large loaf country bread, halved lengthwise

Generous ½ cup (1 stick) unsalted butter, preferably Wilted Herb Butter with Garlic (page 69), at room temperature

Roasted Ugly Garlic (page 64)

Preheat the oven to 400°F. Spread the butter on the open halves of the bread and then drop heaping spoonfuls of the garlic over the top. Close the bread halves and wrap in foil. Bake for 5 minutes and then remove the foil, open up the halves, and bake for another few minutes, until the butter is melted.

SERVES 4 TO 6 /
TIME: ABOUT 1 HR (including roasting the garlic)

PANZANELLA

This classic bread salad is a filling meal with Italian origins.

2 tablespoons extra virgin olive oil

4 cups 2-inch chunks of stale, dry (but not moldy) bread (crusts removed and saved for bread crumbs, page 159)

3 cups vegetable scraps cut into chunks (such as tomatoes, cucumbers), or ½ onion, chopped

1 to 2 cups chopped herb scraps such as parsley, basil, and thyme

½ cup Celery Scrap Pesto (page 58), Carrot Top Pesto (page 51), or other leftover pesto; or ½ cup vinaigrette, or oil and vinegar salad dressing

Salt and pepper, to taste

In a large skillet, heat the oil over medium heat. Add the bread chunks and toast, stirring, for about 10 minutes, until lightly browned. Transfer to a large bowl and add the vegetable scraps and herb scraps. Add the vinaigrette or pesto and toss until coated. Season with salt and pepper. Let sit for at least 30 minutes so flavors can be infused.

SERVES 6–8 / ACTIVE TIME: 30 MIN / INACTIVE TIME: 30 MIN

BREAD PUDDING

The bread pudding method is the same, whether sweet or savory. This recipe is adapted from the leek-Gruyère bread pudding in the December 2006 *Martha Stewart Living* magazine.

3 tablespoons unsalted butter

1 bunch leeks, white and light green parts (save the roots and dark green parts for Vegetable Scrap & Peel Stock, page 230, or for other uses, see page 65)

4 cups half-and-half

2 teaspoons salt

½ teaspoon freshly cracked pepper

5 eggs, lightly beaten in a large metal bowl

1 loaf stale bread (about 1 pound) crusts removed (save for bread crumbs, see Other Ways to Enjoy Old Bread, page 159) and torn into chunks

3 cups mixed grated sharp-flavored hard cheeses, such as Parmesan, Gruyère, and sharp Cheddar

Preheat the oven to 350°F. Melt the butter in a large pan over medium-high heat. Add the leeks and cook for 10 to 15 minutes, until softened. Add the half-and-half, salt, and pepper and bring to a bare simmer.

Whisk 1 cup of this heated mixture into the bowl with the eggs, then pour the entire contents of the bowl back into the pan. Continue to cook the leek-egg-cream mixture over medium heat, stirring continuously, until the mixture has thickened, about 5 minutes.

Layer half of the bread chunks on the bottom of a large casserole dish. Pour 2 cups of the leek mixture over the bread and sprinkle with 1½ cups of the cheeses. Let stand 10 minutes. Arrange the rest of the bread chunks on top and add the rest of the leek-egg mixture, then finish with the remaining cheeses.

Cover the casserole dish with foil and place in a large roasting pan. Add hot water to the roasting pan to come halfway up the side of the casserole dish. Bake until the top is light brown and set, about 1 hour. Remove the foil and bake until deep golden brown, another 15 minutes. Remove from the oven and serve at room temperature.

SERVES 12 / ACTIVE TIME: 1 HR / INACTIVE TIME: 1 HR

WHEAT BRAN ICE CREAM

This sweet treat takes on the toasted nutty flavor of wheat bran. Wheat bran is the skin of the wheat grain. Commercial products such as Raisin Bran cereal and wheat germ include the wheat bran and have higher nutrient and fiber contents than refined flours. However, they also have a number of other additives, including sugar. Recently, pure wheat bran and wheat germ products, such as from Bob's Red Mill, have become available online and in the specialty sections of grocery stores.

2 cups wheat bran (available from Bob's Red Mill)

2½ cups whole milk

2½ cups heavy cream

8 egg yolks

1 cup packed brown sugar

1 tablespoon dark honey

¼ teaspoon kosher salt

Optional garnishes:

a few Leftover Oatmeal Crisps (page 150)

a few tablespoons of Flat Beer Jelly (page 222)

a tablespoon of Black Walnut Puree (page 257)

Preheat the oven to 350°F.

Spread the wheat bran on an 8 × 12-inch baking sheet and toast in the oven for 12 minutes; you will be able to smell the toasting and see a little smoke.

Meanwhile, in a medium saucepan, combine the milk and cream and scrape the toasted wheat bran straight into the pot. Cook over medium-high heat, stirring regularly, until almost boiling. Remove from the heat, cover, and let infuse for 45 minutes.

In a large bowl, whisk together the egg yolks and sugar. Pour the wheat bran infusion into the bowl, whisking continuously. Holding a large medium-mesh strainer over the pot, strain the mixture into the pot. Add the honey and salt and cook over medium heat, gently stirring, until the mixture thickens to coat the back of the spoon, 3 to 4 minutes. Strain in batches through a fine-mesh strainer into a bowl. Chill in the refrigerator for 4 hours, until well chilled.

Transfer to an ice cream maker and follow the manufacturer's instructions.

To serve: Scoop in a bowl with a drizzle of black walnut syrup and a dab of beer jelly. Top with a toasted oatmeal crisp.

TESTER'S NOTE:

It tastes like a toasted nut ice cream, using inexpensive wheat bran. I only had a small strainer, though, so the straining was a bit tedious so that the bran did not go through to the cream. I would recommend using a large (medium-mesh) strainer if you have one.

**MAKES 2 PINTS / ACTIVE TIME: 1 HR /
TOTAL TIME: 6 HRS, includes chilling time**

Opposite: Wheat Bran Ice Cream, drizzled with Black Walnut Puree (page 257) and Flat Beer Jelly (page 222), and topped with Leftover Oatmeal Crisps (page 150).

WHEAT BRAN–HONEY COCKTAIL

1 cup honey
½ cup water
8 cups wheat bran
1 quart rum
Fresh lemon juice
Ice
Angostura bitters

To make the honey syrup, combine the honey and water in a small saucepan and cook over medium heat until the honey is dissolved. Store in a sealed container for a few weeks.

To make the wheat bran rum, preheat the oven to 350°F.

Spread the wheat bran over two 8 × 12-inch baking sheets and toast in the oven for 15 minutes, until browned and smoky. Remove from the oven and let cool.

Combine the toasted bran and rum in a large jar. Cover and let infuse for 2 days.

In batches, strain the rum through a fine mesh strainer, pressing down to extract most of the rum. (Discard the wheat bran solids.) Store the rum in a large mason jar.

For each cocktail, combine ¾ ounce (1½ tablespoons) honey syrup, 2 ounces (¼ cup) wheat bran rum, and ¾ ounce (1½ tablespoons) fresh lemon juice in a shaker. Add ice and shake vigorously until cool to the touch, about 30 seconds. Strain into a lowball or coupe glass, add 4 drops angostura bitters on top, and swirl.

MAKES ENOUGH RUM FOR 15 COCKTAILS / ACTIVE TIME: 30 MIN / INACTIVE TIME: 2 DAYS

Other Ways to Enjoy Old Bread

MEAT LOAF:

Instead of egg, use bread to bind the meat.

CROUTONS:

Dice stale bread and toss on a baking sheet with olive oil, salt, and pepper. Bake at 350°F until golden, about 15 minutes.

BREAD CRUMBS:

Grind dry (but not moldy) bread crusts in a food processor and store for up to 6 months in an airtight container.

SOUP THICKENER:

Instead of flour, use stale bread, most classically in your favorite gazpacho recipe.

DISCARDED BRAN
USED FOR PICKLING

NUKA

IN ADDITION TO brining with salt and pickling with vinegar, I have a lot of respect for the practice of pickling by using bran, the part of the grain that is usually thrown away. I am inspired by the ancient Japanese practice of *nuka,* using discarded rice bran to pickle old wrinkly vegetables such as radishes, eggplant, and cabbages. The vegetables go into the bran dried up, and come out crunchy and pickle-y! Classically, a ceramic pickling vessel, such as one with a drop lid, is used as a "nuka pot," but you can improvise with a pot and use a slightly smaller lid. The main thing is that the nuka needs to be "turned" to condition it first. I like to experiment with using different types of brans such as wheat or buckwheat, and also by pickling unusual things in a nuka, such as roasted ugly potatoes. Serve them with a slice of melted brie inside.

NUKA HOW-TO

Use your hands to make the nuka, but be sure they are washed so that the initial process is clean.

2 pounds rice bran
¼ cup salt
A few scraps of kombu for seasoning and pepper flakes, optional
2 cups water
Vegetable scraps, such as carrot peels, celery leaves, and radish roots
Equipment: ceramic covered pickling pot (the "nuka" pot) that will hold at least 2 quarts of nuka without being full to the top.

Mix the bran, salt, and any seasonings in the pot. Add the water and mix thoroughly. Leave in a cool, dark cupboard for 4 days.

Meanwhile, start to collect your vegetable scraps. You'll need 1 to 2 cups to start. Clean them and rub with salt.

After 4 days, bury the scraps in the nuka to form the initial basis of fermentation. Let ferment, turning the nuka with clean hands daily for 3 days. Pick out and discard the scraps, as they are only used for starter purposes.

Add the scraps or other chunks of vegetables that you want to pickle, such as daikon radishes, Asian cabbages, or even eggplant slices, and continue to turn the nuka every day, checking the vegetables for taste. For a nuka to be fully mature will take 6 months, but you can start eating the vegetables a few days after the initial conditioning.

When the temperatures are warmer, pickling will only take about 12 hours, whereas when it is below 45 degrees, it could take 3 days or more.

The vegetables will become more salty and sour the longer they are left in, so it is best to taste them as they are fermenting so you can adjust for your own temperature, conditions, and taste preferences.

Over time the nuka base will become like the starter "mother" for yogurt, sourdough, or kombucha makers.

5

SEAFOOD

No matter how far I stray from Denmark—a peninsula surrounded by islands—the smell of the sea and the image of the shore and the tidal lands are always with me. This is especially true when I'm cooking.

UNLIKE US SCANDINAVIANS, however, most people only see a fish after it has been "cleaned up" into a fillet—the strip of meat running alongside the backbone—no head, no tail, no guts. (Fish steaks usually contain a little more, as these are cut across the fish, perpendicular to the spine, and include some of the bone.) In fact, almost 50 percent of the seafood supply in the United States is wasted, averaging around 2.3 billion pounds annually. Some 1.3 billion pounds of that is from people who buy and throw out fish and shellfish.

I wish that everyone could see all the parts of a fish and experience just how delicious they can be. (I must admit, I haven't yet figured out a great dish for fish guts. The flavor comes out too strong, and like… guts. I'm still working on it.) That's why I always like to start with the whole fish. It shouldn't be difficult to get a whole fish if you ask your fishmonger.

WHO'S THE BOSS?

LETTING MOTHER NATURE DRIVE SUPPLY—
& DEMAND—FOR SEAFOOD

FOR INDEPENDENT New York fisherman Sean Barrett, meeting the demand for specific types of fresh fish (as opposed to his catch of the day, dictated by Mother Nature) once proved difficult. But this enterprising seaman found a way to solve his supply issue and reduce waste.

Sean is the founder of Dock to Dish, the first community supported fishery (modeled after CSAs, community supported agriculture) in New York State. Dock to Dish allows members to buy fresh fish (and support local fishermen financially) by paying for a share of the local seafood catch at the beginning of the year and then, in their weekly CSA package, they enjoy whatever fish fillet is the catch of the day.

But what to do with the 65 percent of the weight of the fish that is left over after it's filleted? Sean has started to offer this supply, traditionally discarded as waste, to restaurant chefs like Dan Barber, Michael Anthony, Bill Telepan, April Bloomfield, and me, who are keen to support local fishermen like Sean and to cook with less commonly known parts of the fish.

There is also a whole other area of large-scale waste, called *bycatch*. When fish are caught in nets, many more besides the "desirable" fish are caught up in them, and die. These dead fish, the bycatch, are thrown back into the ocean. This is a much larger problem for commercial scale trawlers.

For me, working with this bycatch was like finding a treasure chest. It included *waste fish:* fish considered the bottom of the heap among seafood, such as the Atlantic gurnard (sea robin). Sean tells me that the sea robin has a similarly great flavor and texture to its cousin, the red gurnard (a popular fish in Europe), so now it's in demand.

Ultimately, Sean's inspiring vision is to create a system that reflects the true catch of the day, meaning that, in his words, "the chef isn't the boss. Nature is."

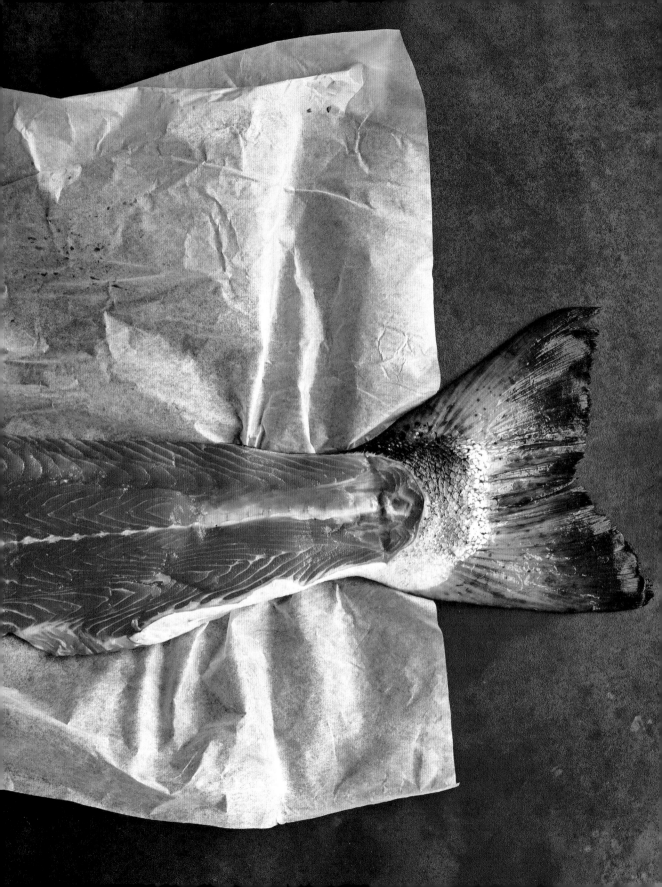

THE BODY, OR TRUNK, OF THE FISH

THE NEXT TIME YOUR fish supplier cuts you a fillet, ask for the rest of the fish. Here's what to do with it.

SCRAPED SALMON TARTARE ON THE BONE

When the fillet is cut from a fish, there is still a lot of good meat left on the main body. Clinging to and in between the bones, and left where the quick fillet knife missed, salmon flesh is tender and sweet. I made this tartare and served it with the Day-Old Charred Garlic Bread (page 154) and a bottle of wine for a casual weekend family-style lunch with friends. The fish gets dressed up with flavors from lots of scraps and condiments from the refrigerator and garden.

3 lemons

1 salmon carcass (see Note)

Assorted chopped herb scraps from the refrigerator (perhaps parsley, chives, chopped dill)

Assorted chopped tender wild herbs and flowering weeds from the backyard garden (lambsquarters, chive flowers, yellow wood sorrel, Asiatic dayflower, garden phlox flowers; see Wild Herbs Glossary, page 269)

Maldon salt and freshly cracked black pepper, to taste

Salty condiments such as Dijon mustard, pickled jalapeños, and cornichons (but don't go out and buy condiments just for this dish!)

Grate the zest from 2 of the lemons and set aside. Cut the zested lemons in half. Cut the unzested lemon into wedges and set aside for serving.

Squeeze the lemon halves all over the salmon carcass and scatter with some of the herbs and all the lemon zest. Finish with a generous sprinkling of Maldon salt and pepper.

To serve, guests help themselves by scraping off a portion of the soft flesh with a spoon, adding a generous extra squeeze of lemon, more herbs, and condiments of choice.

NOTE:

For the salmon carcass (I call it *carcass* because it is what is left of the fish after the fillet has been cut away), buy a whole salmon and ask your fishmonger to fillet the fish (or do it yourself), leaving generous amounts of the pink flesh on the bones. Use your favorite recipe to cook the fillet, and reserve the head and tail for Fish Head & Tail Soup (page 181).

SERVES 4 AS MAIN, more as a first course /
TIME: ABOUT 15 MIN

Scraped Samon Tartare on the Bone (page 169) with
chopped farm herbs and wild weed herbs, charred
garlic bread, and refrigerator-door condiments

GRILLED FISH CARCASSES
WITH MISO-HERB BUTTER

For this cooked dish I prefer a white roundfish (as opposed to flatfish), such as snapper, tilapia, monkfish (check seasonal sustainability; see Resources, page 272).

1 cup (2 sticks) unsalted butter, softened
⅓ cup miso paste
¼ cup chopped herbs, such as thyme, parsley, or rosemary (see Notes)
1 teaspoon kosher salt
4 roundfish carcass halves (see Notes)
Lemon wedges and Maldon salt to taste
Vegetable scraps from the refrigerator that are good for cups, such as white or red cabbage or lettuce
Wild weeds (see page 266) and fresh and wild herbs, such as lemon balm, lemon verbena, wild shiso, baby lambsquarters, for garnish

For the miso-herb butter, in a medium bowl, combine the butter, miso, chopped herbs, and salt until evenly incorporated.

Rub the butter mixture on both sides of the fish carcasses. Keep refrigerated until ready to cook but not overnight.

Heat the grill to high (or set the oven to broil).

Quickly grill or broil both sides of the fish carcasses, turning gently, for about 5 seconds on each side, just until the flesh clinging to the bones is flaky. Remove the fish from the fire, squeeze fresh lemon juice all over, and sprinkle with salt. Serve with the cabbage or lettuce cups and scatter with wild herbs.

NOTES:

Don't go out and buy extra herbs for this. Just use up what you have in the refrigerator or have hanging dried. I choose herbs that are more strongly aromatic and will hold up well after grilling.

For the carcasses, buy 2 whole fish (don't get caught up in exact ounces: Fish come in different sizes and weights. Consider how many people will be eating and eyeball it, or if you feel uncertain, tell your fishmonger you want enough fish for a certain number of people), have the fishmonger fillet the fish (or do it yourself), leaving generous amounts of flesh on the bones. Use your favorite recipe to cook the fillets, and reserve the heads and tails for Fish Head & Tail Soup (page 181).

I like to trim the fish bones but it is not necessary. Using heavy shears, I remove dorsal and underbelly fins so just the center bones remain. This helps the meat slide more easily from the bones.

SERVES 4 / TIME: ABOUT 30 MIN

Opposite: Grilled Fish Carcasses with Miso-Herb Butter, chopped herbs, vegetable scraps, and wild herbs

SOMETHING'S FISHY: TIPS ON SMELLING, TASTING, STORING, & EATING WHOLE FISH

A FRESH FISH...

- Has a smooth (not sticky) texture.
- Has flat (not bulging) eyes.
- Does not have a fishy odor. Fishiness in taste is a subjective judgment and some oilier fish, such as bluefish, mackerel, and anchovies, will naturally taste deeper and more fish-flavorful.

A NOT-SO-FRESH FISH...

- Has a very fishy, "off," sour, or ammonia-like odor. (This means you need to throw it out.)

If you are not going to use fish within 2 days of purchase, the U.S. Food and Drug Administration recommends you freeze it. To protect it, wrap it tightly in plastic wrap and then foil. Raw fish will last 2 to 6 months in the freezer. Cooked fish will last 4 to 6 months in the freezer. You may also try one of the longer-lasting options like drying or fermenting (see page 9 and 10).

A note on eating raw fish: There are several recipes that contain raw fish in this book. The FDA recommends that all fish that will be eaten raw be frozen first in order to kill parasites. It is still safer to eat fish that has been cooked.

Let your fishmonger or grocer know if you plan to eat the fish raw and buy the best quality they have—the freshest and from the cleanest environment.

The Whole Fish: Buying and Preparing

In Asian restaurants, whole fish are brought to the table on a large platter with a dramatic flourish, the same way a prime rib or rack of lamb might be at a steakhouse. Whole fish is much preferred to fillets because the flesh on the bone retains the moisture and flavor. Plus the omega-3 health benefits of the fatty layer next to the skin and the cartilage are beginning to be more widely appreciated.

What's more, buying a whole fish is much more economical than buying fillets. The fishmonger at the grocery store will gut, scale (ask for the scales to fry, page 192), and clean the fish for you. Following are two simple ways to cook whole fish deliciously: steaming and frying. A note on sustainability: When making your selection, bear in mind that many fish species are endangered and/or overfished. Obtaining high-quality fish also takes into consideration the environment it came from as well as methods of production and harvest. Ask questions of, and develop a good relationship with, your fishmonger. See the Resources section (page 272) for information about sustainable seafood choices.

BASIC WAY TO STEAM WHOLE FISH

Enhance delicate steamed fish with aromatic flavors
like ginger, green onions, and coriander.

**1 small whole fish, gutted and cleaned (it doesn't
really matter the poundage; it is more important
that you get what is fresh and in season and is
small enough to fit in your pot)**
1 teaspoon grated fresh ginger
⅓ cup tamari soy sauce
⅓ cup mirin (rice wine)

Place the fish in a heatproof bowl inside a steamer
or rice cooker and spoon the ginger, tamari, and mirin
over the top. Cover and steam for 10 minutes, until
the fish is flaky and still moist. Serve the fish in the
bowl and let guests serve themselves by scooping off
the flesh from the bone on one side and then flipping
the fish and scooping off the flesh from the other.
Accompany with hot bowls of rice and some stir-fried
greens.

SERVES 4 / TIME: 15 MIN

BASIC WAY TO FRY WHOLE FISH

The main equipment needed here is a wok or pot large
enough to fry the fish so that it becomes crispy. Make
a spicy sauce, like a black bean garlic or Korean sweet
chili sauce, or a thick, sweet-and-sour tangy sauce, to
serve with the fish.

**1 whole small whitefish, such as trout or flounder,
gutted and cleaned**
Flour or cornstarch for dredging
Neutral vegetable or rice bran oil, for frying

Rinse the fish and pat dry. Make cuts in the fish flesh
through to the bone about 2 inches apart on both
sides so that the frying oil can make it crispy. Dredge
the entire fish (including the cuts) in the flour or
cornstarch.

Heat 3 inches of oil in a wok or Dutch oven to 300°F.
(Use a frying thermometer, or test by throwing in a tiny
piece of fish or flour; it is hot enough if it immediately
sizzles and crackles.) Slowly slide the fish into the
oil, and fry, spooning oil over the top, for 1 minute.
Remove the fish. Increase the heat under the oil. Turn
the fish and carefully slide it in again to fry on the
other side for another 2 minutes, until the outside of
the fish is golden brown. Serve in the middle of the
table on a serving platter, spooning the sauce partially
over the top. Accompany with rice, pickles, and
sautéed greens.

SERVES 4 / TIME: 15 MIN

FISH HEADS & TAILS

IN THE UNITED STATES fish heads are considered byproducts. But the head of a fish contains a lot of the animal's most nutritious and tasty oils and fat. In other cultures, the best part of the fish is the head, and the cheeks are offered as a tribute to honored guests. The tail and bones of smaller fish (we are not imagining you trying to fry the tail of a tuna or swordfish) can be dredged in flour and shallow fried in a sauté pan for 2 minutes on each side, making it crispy and great as a snack with a squeeze of lemon and herbs or dip. Larger fish heads and tails can be used in soups or curries as follows.

TNW

FISH HEAD CURRY SAUCE

Make the coconut base curry ahead of time or use leftover curry sauce. Serve with fresh herbs and steamed rice.

3 tablespoons sesame oil
1 tablespoon chopped fresh lemongrass
1 tablespoon chopped fresh chili
2 tablespoons chopped fresh ginger
2 cloves garlic, minced
1 teaspoon ground turmeric
A few cups pre-cooked potato, radish, and/or eggplant chunks
Head from a large fish (see Note)
Juice of 1 lime
½ cup coconut milk
Fresh Asian herbs such as Thai basil and coriander, for garnish (optional)

In a large pot or wok, heat the oil over high heat. Add the lemongrass, chili, ginger, garlic, and turmeric and stir for a few minutes, until fragrant.

Add 2 to 3 cups water and bring to a boil. Add the vegetables and fish head, adding more water if needed so the head is covered. Reduce the heat and simmer for 10 minutes, until flesh is tender and cooked. Stir in the lime juice and coconut milk and heat until warmed through. Garnish with fresh herbs, if you like.

NOTE:
Smaller fish heads do not have as much flesh and are more suited for a fish stock.

SERVES 4–8 / TIME: 45 MIN (including pre-cooking)

FISH HEAD & TAIL SOUP

Instead of adding vegetables to a fish stock, this recipe adds fish to a tomato stock, also called a tomato dashi.

2 large heads and tails from fish such as haddock, snapper, or salmon

4 cups Tomato Broth (Dashi) (page 136), plus 2 cups of its leftover tomato pulp

1 cup cooked barley or other grain (or leftovers)

Liberal amounts of chopped fresh lemony herbs, such as lemon verbena or shiso

Kosher salt and freshly ground black pepper, to taste

Lemon halves

Heat a grill to high heat. Grill the fish heads and tails until the skin is lightly charred and the flesh is flaky, 2 minutes on each side for the tails and 5 minutes on each side for the heads. There is an art to this, and you must watch carefully, because grills will differ in heat and fish heads differ in size and relative structure and leanness. So pay more attention to doneness and less to the times.

In a large pot, heat the tomato dashi, and bring to a bare simmer. Add the tomato pulp, barley, fish heads and tails, and herbs, adding water if needed so that the fish is just covered. Cook until warmed through.

Season to taste with salt and pepper and squeezes of lemon. Remove the heads and tails. Ladle the remaining soup into bowls, adding small pieces of flesh from the heads to top each serving.

SERVES 4 / TIME: 45 MIN

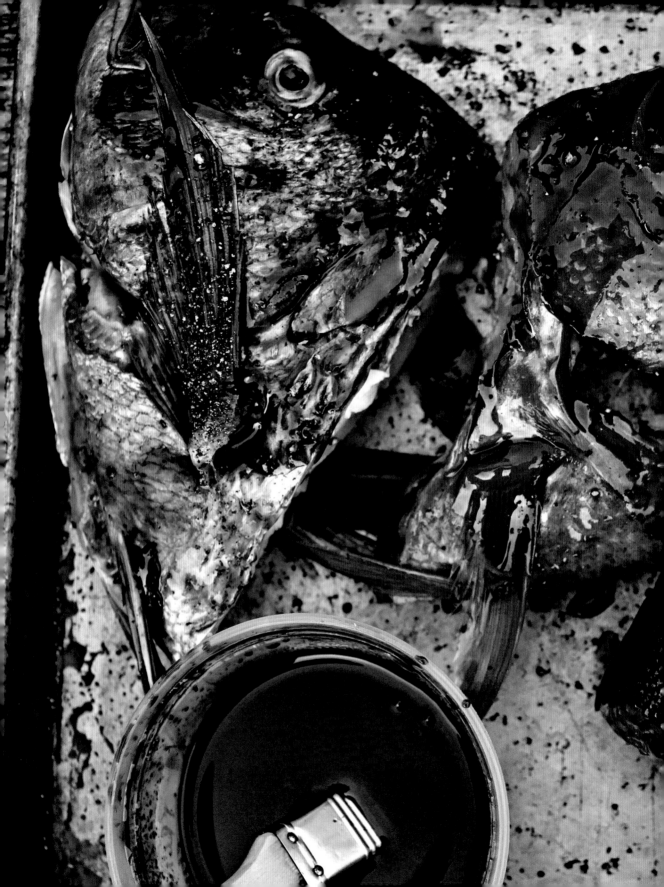

FISH COLLARS

THE COLLAR OF A LARGE FISH, such as cod, is the part between the head and the body; it has a (healthy omega-3) fatty richness that is ultra satisfying.

SWEET & SALTY FISH COLLARS

The collar is one of my favorite parts of the fish. Baste it with naturally sweet and salty flavor from briny konbu and dark sweet prunes. The briny and sweet sauce is easy to make ahead and store in the refrigerator.

3 cups prunes (dried up from old ugly plums or hardened in the pantry is fine)

3 (8 × 3-inch) pieces (about ½ sheet) dried konbu

4 to 8 collars from cod (sourced from George Bank), bass, or other large fish collars, about 3 pounds (see **Note**)

Fill a large pot with 6 cups water and bring to a boil. Add the prunes and konbu and cook over medium heat for 45 minutes. Strain and return the liquid to the pot. (Discard the prunes and konbu, or reserve for other use. Keep in mind that the prunes might have a slightly briny taste.) Turn the heat to low and simmer for another 30 minutes, until the sauce thickens and reduces to a deeper flavored syrup. You should have about 2 cups.

Heat a grill (preferably with hickory) until the grate is at high heat. (Alternatively you can set the oven to broil and cook them the same way on aluminum foil.) Brush the collars with the sauce. Grill (or broil), basting frequently with the sauce, for 2–3 minutes, checking to make sure the collar is seared and golden on one side and then flipping and searing on the other side for another 1–2 minutes, until just cooked. Remove immediately and serve with sauce on the side.

NOTE:
Ask your fishmonger for leftover fish collars. If using cod, know that stocks of Atlantic cod have been depleted due to unsustainable fishing methods, so choose Pacific cod or Alaskan walleye pollock.

SERVES 4 / TIME: 1 HR 15 MIN

Previous spread: Fish heads with sweet and salty glaze (above)

FISH SKIN

THE SKIN IS NOT ONLY one of the most healthy and vitamin-rich parts of the fish, it's also delicious. The crispy, crunchy, and often juicy skin—which is usually discarded before the fish is even displayed for sale—is better than a potato chip. Get used to leaving it on the fish or cooking with it alone.

CRISPY SALMON WITH SKIN

This dish makes salmon the way it should be, with crispy skin, never dried out, since it cooks the layer of fat next to the skin and about one inch of flesh. Serve with Charred Wrinkled Cucumbers (page 120) and Brined Cucumber Peels (page 120).

Skin of 1 salmon steak or fillet, roughly cut off, leaving 1 inch of flesh
Kosher salt and freshly ground black pepper
Fresh herbs, such as dill or mint, and peas in the pod

Preheat a grill (or oiled saucepan) to medium high. The alternative to a grill for this recipe is to pan-roast the salmon, since there will be no risk of it drying out. The skin seals in the moisture and the omega-3 oils from the subcutaneous (under the skin) fat.

Season the salmon skin with salt and pepper. Place it on the hot grill (pan) skin side down first, for 5 minutes, until the skin is crispy and edges turn up. Turn the salmon and grill for another 3 minutes, until the flesh is tender and flaky. Serve with fresh herbs or peas.

MAKES ONE STEAK PER PERSON / TIME: 15 MIN

Opposite: Crispy Salmon with Skin and Brined Cucumber Peels, Herb Oil, and Horseradish Buttermilk Dressing

PUFFED FISH SKINS

This is another way to cook fish skins, but this time there is no flesh, so the skin puffs up like a chip. It is a three-step process of brining, dehydrating, and then frying, but you can make batches and freeze them for later. For serving as a snack, I sprinkle them with seaweed vinegar powder. I like the acidity of the vinegar.

Yield will depend on how large a fish you have the skin from, or how many skins you can collect from your fishmonger. Try to get enough skin for an 11 × 8-inch baking sheet or rack, to make one batch of between 10 and 20 skins.

Large salmon or other fish skin, without flesh (ask your fishmonger to remove it for you, or peel it off a cooked salmon). Try to get enough to spread across an 11 × 8-inch sheet.

Salt for brine

Oil for frying

(Optional) powders for finishing with different flavors: I like seaweed vinegar powder

For a large batch: Make the brine by combining ¼ cup salt and 2 quarts water; stir until the salt is dissolved. Add the fish and brine at room temperature for a minimum of 2 hours (or up to overnight).

For a smaller batch: Bring a large pot of salted water to a boil. Add the skin and boil for 2 to 3 minutes. Remove and clean off any remaining bits of flesh.

Use a dehydrator at 150°F, or preheat the oven to 150°F. After brining, lightly sponge the salt off the skins, lay them out flat on a wire rack or sheet with holes (see Note). Dry in the dehydrator or oven for 2 hours. When done, the skin will still feel slightly viscous and pliable, not completely dry and crackly.

Cut the sheet into 2-inch squares. You can freeze the skins at this point if you made a large batch, but of course you can fry them immediately.

To fry, heat at least 1 inch oil in a deep fryer or saucepan over high heat. In batches if necessary, drop the skins into the hot oil and fry for 35 seconds, until crispy and puffy. Remove with a slotted spoon and lay on paper towels to remove any excess cooking oil.

NOTE:

If you use a sheet for dehydrating, the sheet must have holes, or the skins will stick.

TESTER'S NOTE:

I put the skin on solid baking sheets first, and that's when I found out you must have a wire rack instead. Frying, it only took a second or two to puff up and it tasted a bit briny but not fishy or slimy at all.

ACTIVE TIME: 45 MIN / INACTIVE TIME: 4 HRS or more

FISH SCALES & BLOODLINE

EATING FISH SCALES SOUNDS CRAZY, like eating some kind of metal armor. Eating fish bloodline sounds just about as appealing. Trust that when done right, they are really good. I'm not talking about eating a chunk of bloodline or a plate piled high with nothing but fish scales! But they add pizzazz to a more bland meal, shaved or sprinkled on top.

TILEFISH TARTARE WITH FISH SCALES, CAPERS, & HERBS

This is very simple to make. I like the textures: the crunchiness of the fish scales and the softness of the tartare and capers. Fish, acidity, herbs, and crunch. I love that combination.

3–4 fillets (total 24 ounces) of tilefish (or fluke), sliced and diced (must be fresh; see Note about raw fish on page 175)
Drizzle of grapeseed oil
1 tablespoon capers
Minced fresh chives or green onions
Juice of 1 lemon
Black pepper
1 cup Fried Fish Scales (page 192)

In a medium bowl, combine the fish, oil, capers, and chives.

Season liberally with lemon juice and pepper and top with the crunchy fish scales.

SERVES 4, as a first course or light meal /
TIME: 15 MIN

Opposite: Tilefish Tartare with Fish Scales, Capers & Herbs (page 189) **This page:** Whisk the fish scales; see page 192.

FRIED FISH SCALES

These are great. Crunchy—not poky or bony—plus, I suspect, full of calcium. Use your creativity: Imagine them as well as a great crunchy topping for a fish casserole or on a hollandaise sauce for fish. Because scales are often the first parts of the fish to be removed and discarded, it can be difficult to find them. Japanese restaurants, however, can be good resources. Ask them for the scales they are throwing away.

2 cups neutral oil, for deep frying
1 cup fish scales, from black sea bass, salmon, or Pacific cod
¼ teaspoon kosher salt
½ lemon, for serving
Chopped parsley, for serving

Heat the oil in a wok or deep pot over high heat. Add the fish scales and fry, continuously whisking so that the scales do not clump together, for 3 to 5 minutes, until crispy. Drain and sprinkle with the salt, a generous squeeze of lemon, and a sprinkling of parsley.

MAKES 1 CUP / TIME: 10 MIN

CURED TUNA BLOODLINE

What is the fish's *bloodline*? It is the darker muscle section of fillets or steaks of fish like tuna, mackerel, and swordfish. The bloodline is richer and tastes "fishier" than the other parts of the fish flesh and is often cut away before selling to consumers. I like it cured because it lasts well and you only need a little: Just as you would with a truffle, you can shave thin slivers of the cured bloodline over simple flavored dishes, including the Beet Pulp Wide Pasta (page 31). If you are not able to obtain bloodline by asking your fishmonger, look for other cured tuna products online, such as the Spanish *mojama* or the Italian *mosciame*.

1 bloodline, carved from a tuna steak or a fillet (you'll get about ¼ pound from a 2-pound tuna steak)
Kosher salt

Pack the bloodline in enough salt to cover, and leave for 2 days. Rinse off the salt, then smoke in a smoker at a low temperature (70–90°F) or hang to dry for several weeks. It will keep for months, wrapped well in plastic wrap in the refrigerator.

SERVES 10 or more, from shavings as flavor additive / TIME: 1 MONTH

AGENT OF FLAVOR:
CURED FISH

IF YOU HAVE MORE FISH than you can eat or you run out of time to cook it, you can pack it in salt, as people have done for centuries. After fish is cured, it lasts a long time and can be sliced very thinly and served topped with herbs, lemon, and pickles.

Cured fish products are also great flavoring agents. Think of them as truffles. An entire truffle would be much too strong to consider popping in your mouth or eating whole on a plate. It is meant to be shaved over something very simple to impart umami—deep richness—or added to oils to infuse them with flavor. A local fishmonger I know says his way to use cured fish is in things like beef stew because it brings out the base notes of the flavor. Salted fish is also used to make fish sauce and smoked and pickled fish.

If curing or smoking fish isn't for you, an easy way to begin experiencing the flavor punch of dried fish is by purchasing small packets of bonito or katsuobushi, available as flakes or small shavings in Asian and specialty groceries as well as online. Small shavings can be used to impart flavor to mild dishes; for example, use a teaspoon as a topping for cold tofu with sesame-soy dressing. The traditional Japanese dashi, which is the base for sauces, soups, and much of Japanese cuisine, is made with bonito flakes combined in water with dried kelp (konbu), heated and then strained. (Dashi is used in this book, and by most chefs today, in a broader sense than the original, which just used tuna flakes.)

A second way to experience the flavor is to purchase some good quality fish sauce. Use it instead of salt to add salty flavor plus something more to vegetables, stews, and curries.

6

MEAT: PUTTING IT TO THE SIDE

This chapter is the shortest in the book. I don't use very much meat in my cooking because I think there is already so much of it—too much. I like to feel light after a meal, and that's hard to do after you've eaten a giant burger.

TO BE FAIR, MEAT is a food that is less frequently wasted by consumers because it isn't cheap. The reason for its relatively high cost is that producing meat uses (and wastes) a lot of resources: water, electricity, fuel… and the list goes on. To produce one hamburger, for example, it takes the same amount of water as a 90-minute shower. One way to reduce such waste is to eat meat less frequently and in smaller portions.

For centuries, meat was considered a luxury by civilizations around the world. In some cultures, it still is, and they have dishes for different parts of the animal, nose to tail. My approach to meat isn't much different. I look at the whole animal, consider all of its parts, and figure out how each one will taste best.

Plucking a freshly killed Mountain Meadow farm chicken over ice

CHICKEN & EGGS WITH
CHICKEN INNARDS & SKIN SAUCE

Start with one chicken, a whole chicken, the best quality you can find (free range, running around eating beetles and seeds) to get real flavor. It's even better if it isn't packaged in parts, as a whole chicken is more beautiful and more economical. But remember that even a "whole" chicken in the market isn't really whole. It is missing the feet, head, and feathers, but will often contain the inner organs. Check with your farmer or butcher to be sure.

Roasted Chicken

1 whole 3- to 4-pound chicken

1 lemon, quartered

3 rosemary sprigs

1 tablespoon vegetable oil

2 teaspoons kosher salt

Chicken Innards and Skin Sauce

2 tablespoons, plus ½ cup (1 stick) unsalted butter

Chicken kidneys, liver, and heart from the chicken cavity (often referred to as *giblets*, along with the neck and the gizzard)

1 shallot, finely chopped

1 bunch parsley stems, chopped (keep the leaves for serving)

Leaves from 6 sprigs thyme

2 tablespoons lemon juice

½ teaspoon kosher salt

Poached Eggs

2 tablespoons white distilled vinegar

2 teaspoons kosher salt

4 to 6 eggs (one per person)

To Serve

Parsley leaves

½ teaspoon kosher salt

Freshly ground black pepper

2 tablespoons lemon juice

Wild herbs: lambsquarter, shiso

To roast the chicken: Preheat the oven to 400°F. Stuff the cavity of the chicken with the quartered lemon and rosemary. Brush the outside of the chicken with the oil and sprinkle with the salt. Place in a roasting pan and roast for 1 hour, until the juices run clear.

To start the sauce: In a small pan, melt the 2 tablespoons butter over medium-high heat. Add the kidneys, liver, and heart and the shallot and sauté for about 5 minutes, until lightly browned. Add the parsley stems and the thyme and stir for another minute. Transfer to a blender and set aside.

When the chicken is done, let it rest for about 15 minutes.

To finish the sauce: Spoon the juices from the bottom of the roasting pan, scraping up the fatty and brown bits from the bottom, and transfer to the blender. Remove the skin from the chicken and add to the blender. Dice the remaining 1 stick butter and add to the blender along with the lemon juice and salt. Blend on high, until smooth.

To poach the eggs: Fill a wide saucepan halfway with water and add the vinegar and salt. Bring to a boil and then reduce the heat so that the water is gently simmering. Crack one egg into a small bowl. Gently pour the egg into the water, following with the other eggs. Poach for about 5 minutes, until the whites of the eggs are just set.

To serve: Roughly shred the breast and other meat into large chunks, and arrange on a serving platter, with the wings and thighs.

With a large slotted spoon, gently remove each egg from the pan and set on top of the chicken chunks. Top with the skin and innards sauce and finish with the parsley leaves, salt, pepper, and lemon to taste. I also like to use baby lambsquarters and shiso leaves to finish.

NOTE:
Save the bones and gristly leftovers to make a nice chicken stock (page 231).

SERVES 4 TO 6 / TIME: ABOUT 1½ HRS

BLOOD

ALTHOUGH CONSUMING BLOOD may make you think of vampires, blood and blood products are eaten the world over. In Asia, blood is cooked as a pudding that is sliced, and in the United Kingdom the pudding made with blood is known as black pudding. Italy, Spain, and Africa use blood in their traditional cuisines. American Indians and farmers took the fresh blood from deer. Blood adds thickness and flavor to a dish, and is for the most part wasted when animals are slaughtered. Blood can be used as an iron-rich substitute for eggs in baking at a ratio of 65 grams of blood for 1 egg.

The color and viscosity of blood is beautiful.

Joe Yardley making
blood sausage

BLOOD SAUSAGE

I like to serve a blood sausage with red cabbage and fruity vinegar. The colors are so striking together and the flavors are so complementary. Then it's an easy feat to empty the sausage contents from the casings and sauté with some red cabbage scraps. Drizzle with some salted plum vinegar. In addition to the pig's blood and pork casings (see Notes), you'll need a large funnel (8 inches minimum) and butcher's twine for tying the sausage links.

Thanks to Joe Yardley, chef de cuisine at New York's Agern, for demonstrating the step-by-step method below.

20 feet pork casings (see Notes)

1 gallon pig's blood, fresh from the butcher (see Notes)

3½ cups day-old (or even a few days old) cooked rice

4 cups beet pulp (leftover from home juicing or from a local juice bar) or beet juice

½ cup mixed spices (I use about 4 tablespoons allspice and 4 tablespoons cloves)

2 turns cracked black pepper

Kosher salt

Soak the casings in a bowl of warm water so that they remain pliable and ready for stuffing.

In a large bowl, combine the blood, rice, beet pulp, spices, pepper, and salt.

Attach the top of the casings to the bottom of the funnel and place a large metal bowl at the other end of the casings to collect any residue of drippings that miss the casing. Ladle the blood mixture into the funnel and ease down into the casing. When the casing is stuffed, tie off the length with butcher's twine into separate joints of 6 to 8 inches. Since they contain liquid blood, the sausages will feel looser than meat sausage.

Bring a large pot of water to a simmer, but not a boil (160° to 170°F). Gently poach the sausage in the water for 15 minutes, until firm. Remove and cool immediately. Let dry.

Pan-fry, slice, or smoke using your favorite sausage recipe.

NOTES:

I used pig's blood but other animal blood can be used. It just has to be fresh and refrigerated, as it coagulates after one day. Pork casings are available from the butcher's section of the market.

MAKES ABOUT 5 LBS. OF SAUSAGES / TIME: 2 HRS

Opposite: Blood Sausage with red cabbage and salted plum vinegar (umeboshi)

Opposite: Blood sausage how-to
demonstration: Joe Yardley

7

DAIRY: THE MANY FACES OF MILK

For centuries most cultures considered milk a precious drink, and so each one (with the exception of East Asian cuisines) developed ways to conserve, ferment, and use all of its parts.

FRESH MILK GENERALLY COMES from cows, goats, sheep, or yaks. Before modern commercial pasteurization and homogenization, raw milk would have a thick layer of cream on top, which was skimmed off to make butter and buttermilk. The remaining skimmed milk was used as the basis for making hard cheese—through a process of salting, drying, and aging—which would last the winter.

As milk ages, the proteins that keep it smooth and creamy start to bind and clump, or curdle, and it begins to separate into curds and whey. Don't automatically throw it out if this happens. The curds are the lumps, and the whey is the thin liquid. (The same curdling effect can be created by adding lemon juice and vinegar to milk to make a rustic home version of ricotta cheese or paneer.) Curds and whey may look unappetizing, but that does not necessarily mean the milk is spoiled. Curds are the basis for making fresh cottage cheese. The liquidy whey is used in a variety of dishes and is a staple of Nordic cuisine.

After the separation into curds and whey has occurred, milk may begin to turn "sour," i.e., it tastes a little off, but it can still be used in baking. Milk need not be thrown away until it is spoiled: It will smell bad or start to collect mold. Milk is also fermented (not curdled) into yogurt, which coagulates based on the action of two lactobacilli (good bacteria). Whey can also be fermented into kefir, a yogurt-y drink found mainly in Eastern Europe.

Too-old yogurt

YOGURT

THERE ARE SO MANY WAYS to enjoy yogurt other than in a cup with jam. Part of the reason yogurt is so wonderful to work with is that it doesn't spoil easily. It can last 2 to 3 weeks unopened in the fridge. Just check to make sure it has not gone moldy. Yogurt can also be frozen and used in baking.

SALTED YOGURT

Yogurt is not just a sweet breakfast food, with berries or jam stirred up from the bottom of a prepackaged container. Add some salt to yogurt and it has a tang that is a great marinade for meats, or as a savory dip topped with some fresh herbs such as mint or dill.

2 cups yogurt (past expiration date is OK)
2 tablespoons extra virgin olive oil
1 tablespoon Maldon salt
Freshly cracked black pepper

Mix the yogurt, oil, and salt together in a small bowl. Garnish with pepper and serve.

MAKES 2 CUPS / TIME: 5 MIN

WHIPPED YOGURT

This chilled yogurt is like a fluffy cloud; it works well in the Carrot Top Granita (page 49) as well as other light desserts.

1 cup heavy cream
2 egg yolks
2 tablespoons sugar
1 gelatin sheet (I recommend leaf gelatin sheets
with 200 bloom for the most consistent firmness),
softened in cold water for a few minutes
2 cups plain yogurt

In a medium saucepan, heat the cream over medium heat for 5 minutes, until hot to the touch. In a large bowl, mix the egg yolks and sugar, then whisk in the heated cream. Once incorporated, pour the contents of the bowl back into the pot. Cook over medium heat, stirring continuously, for 3 minutes, until the mixture is slightly thickened and coats the back of a wooden spoon.

Squeeze out any excess water from the gelatin and whisk into the warm custard. Pour the custard into a bowl and fold in the yogurt. Chill in the refrigerator for at least 30 minutes.

Right before serving, whip the yogurt mixture with a mixer for 1 to 2 minutes, until light and fluffy.

MAKES 4 1-CUP SERVINGS / TIME: 1 HR

BUTTERMILK

OLD-FASHIONED BUTTERMILK was originally the liquid that was left over when cream was churned into butter. The leftover liquid would sit around and the natural bacteria in it would cause it to slightly sour. This buttermilk is also what Nordic countries refer to as unrefrigerated sour milk that has not been pasteurized. Today buttermilk made by fermentation is considered extremely healthy because it contains probiotics and bacteria beneficial to the gut.

In the U.S. today you can buy *cultured buttermilk* in the grocery store. Cultured buttermilk is made from pasteurized cow's milk, which is inoculated with a lactis culture that ferments the lactose in the milk into lactic acid. This buttermilk can be used as a starter to make more by using 1 part buttermilk to 4 parts whole milk.

You can make your own buttermilk by letting filtered raw milk sit at a warm room temperature for about 12 hours until it *clabbers*, which means to thicken and curdle. The entire liquid is buttermilk, but if you desire a thicker product you can strain off the thinner liquid and use it for any recipe that requires whey. (Clabber was used in the South as a kind of oatmeal with brown sugar and cinnamon and also substituted for baking soda in baked goods.)

But note that raw milk is prohibited in some states. If you don't have access to it, another way to make buttermilk is to use sour milk or to add 1 tablespoon lemon juice or vinegar to 1 cup whole or 2 percent milk and let it stand until it curdles (about 15 minutes), and you have your own buttermilk.

BUTTERMILK-HORSERADISH DRESSING

The gentle sour flavor of buttermilk provides a nice contrast to the punch of horseradish. Make this dressing at least one day before serving and store in the refrigerator for up to a week. Use as a dressing in Cabbage Stem Salad with Buttermilk-Horseradish Dressing on page 40; with roasted vegetables such as cauliflower (see Other Ways to Enjoy Cauliflower Scraps on page 55) or grilled leek tops (see Other Ways to Enjoy Leeks on page 65); and for salads, meats, and as a dip.

1 cup buttermilk
2 tablespoons horseradish (I use freshly grated,
    but bottled is OK)
½ cup heavy cream
1 tablespoon lemon juice
1 teaspoon kosher salt
Freshly cracked black pepper

In a medium mixing bowl, combine the buttermilk and horseradish. Cover and refrigerate for at least 2 to 3 hours to let the flavors infuse. It will taste a bit sour and spicy at the same time. (If using fresh horseradish, strain the buttermilk and discard the solids.)

In the chilled stainless steel bowl of a mixer, whip the heavy cream until it forms semi-stiff peaks.

To the buttermilk, add the lemon juice, salt, and pepper and stir to combine. Gently fold in the whipped cream until fully incorporated into the buttermilk.

To serve, freshen with more lemon juice, salt, and pepper to taste.

MAKES 1½ CUPS / ACTIVE TIME: 25 MIN /
TOTAL TIME: 2½ HRS

WHEY

TRUE WHEY is the thin, yellowy liquid resulting from the separation of curdled milk. You may be familiar with it if you've ever made cheese and produced a separated liquid in the process. If you are not planning to become your own fresh cheesemaker and therefore do not have a source for whey or curds, it is still easy to produce curds and whey at home by curdling milk: Heat 4 cups whole milk and ½ teaspoon salt to 165° to 185°F (about 12 minutes at medium-high heat) and add 2 tablespoons vinegar. The milk will curdle and separate into curds and whey. You'll have about 1 cup solids (curds) and 2½ cups liquids (whey). Use the curds as a substitute for cottage cheese or paneer cheese in any recipe that is not too strict about consistency. The whey can be used to make cocktails (below), in the Brussels Sprout Stems & Leaves recipe (page 39), or as a substitute for milk in baking recipes.

ORANGE WHEY TEQUILA COCKTAIL

This cocktail creation by bartender Michael Reynolds, owner of the Black Crescent bar in New York City, uses an orange zest–infused whey in a savory, slightly spicy version of a tequila sour. It tastes a little like a spiked version of a Creamsicle.

1 ounce (2 tablespoons) Orange Zest Whey (at right)
1 ounce (2 tablespoons) tequila
1 ounce (2 tablespoons) ancho chili liqueur
    (Ancho Reyes)
¾ ounce (1½ tablespoons) lime juice
Ice

In a cocktail shaker, combine the whey, tequila, liqueur, and lime juice. Add ice and shake vigorously for 30 seconds, until the shaker is thoroughly chilled. Strain into a coupe cocktail glass and serve.

**MAKES 1 COCKTAIL / ACTIVE TIME: 5 MIN /
TOTAL TIME: OVERNIGHT**

ORANGE ZEST WHEY

2 (1-inch-wide) strips orange zest (removed
    with a vegetable peeler)
2 cups whey (see above)

In a small sealable jar, combine the orange strips and whey. Refrigerate for 12 to 24 hours. Strain through a fine mesh strainer.

**MAKES 2 CUPS, enough for 8 cocktails /
ACTIVE TIME: 5 MIN / TOTAL TIME: AT LEAST 12 HRS**

CHEESE RINDS

CHEESE RINDS ARE A common leftover after grating blocks of Parmesan, Gruyère, pecorino, or other flavorful hard cheeses. These rinds add delicious but not overpowering flavor to all sorts of dishes.

PARMESAN RIND BROTH

This broth is like cheese dashi. The slow simmer allows the rinds to infuse the water with cheesiness. I used it as a base for different soups, for a chawanmushi–style custard replacing the corn dashi in the Corn Kernel Flan (page 147), and for sauces.

½ pound **Parmesan cheese rinds** (about 1 cup rinds),
  broken into 2-inch chunks
4 cups water
1 teaspoon kosher salt
1 tablespoon lemon juice

Combine the rinds and water in a medium pot. Bring to a boil, reduce the heat, and simmer for 1 hour, until the liquid is reduced to about 2 cups. Remove the rinds. Add the salt and lemon juice and refrigerate for up to 5 days.

MAKES 2 CUPS / TIME: 1 HR

SALTED FISH CARPACCIO WITH PARMESAN RIND BROTH & PICKLED GREEN ALMONDS

This dish uses the Parmesan Rind Broth just as a flavoring, not as a soup. Note: When purchasing fish for carpaccio, tartare, or sushi, tell the grocer that you plan to eat the fish raw, and let him or her recommend the freshest and most suitable fillet available. If the grocer is filleting it for you, ask to have the parts wrapped separately: the fillet, the skin with the underlayer of fat still clinging to it (for grilling), and the head and tail for the recipes on page 181. They might even have the scales for the recipe on page 192.

½ cup kosher salt

1 teaspoon black peppercorns

1 teaspoon coriander seeds

1 teaspoon fennel seeds

1 teaspoon dill seeds

1 teaspoon chopped rosemary

1 teaspoon finely chopped thyme

1 pound very fresh whitefish fillet (haddock, fluke, snapper, or sustainable cod)

Pickled Green Almonds (page 262)

1 teaspoon lemon juice

2 tablespoons Parmesan Rind Broth (page 213)

Drizzle of grapeseed oil

Edible flowers (optional)

In a small bowl, mix the salt with the peppercorns, all the seeds, the rosemary, and thyme. Spread evenly over the fillet, massaging the mix into the flesh; turn over and spread over the other side. Wrap with plastic wrap on a dish and refrigerate for 24 hours.

Completely wipe the salt from the fillet but don't rinse.

With a sharp knife, slice the fillet very thinly so the pieces look almost translucent, being sure to cut on the bias and against the grain.

Top the slices of fillet with a few slices of pickled almonds and sprinkle with salt. Drizzle with the lemon juice, Parmesan broth, and grapeseed oil. Scatter with small edible flowers if you like.

SERVES 4 / ACTIVE TIME: 30 MIN / TOTAL TIME: 24 HRS

S

DRINKS
& DREGS

Whether you prefer coffee, tea, beer, or wine, there is often still something good left in the coffeemaker, tea bag, bottle, or can.

COFFEE GROUNDS

COFFEE IS NOT REALLY a bean, but rather the seed of the coffee plant, a small tree or shrub that grows in warm climates. The seed is the inside "stone" of the coffee berry, the edible burgundy-colored fruit that is discarded in order to process the seed. About 10 billion pounds of coffee beans are produced every year and, once ground and brewed into a coffee drink, the leftover grounds are discarded, sometimes to be composted or used as mulch, but often not.

I started thinking about the waste from coffee because in a restaurant people drink a lot of coffee; you can end up throwing away a lot of coffee grounds. We decided to start cooking with used coffee grounds, and the dishes we came up with tasted just as good—with a rich dark coffee flavor—as they would have using fresh coffee grounds. Just store the grounds in the refrigerator in a sealed plastic container with enough space for air circulation.

COFFEE GROUNDS PANNA COTTA

2 sheets gelatin (I prefer leaf gelatin 200 bloom),
   or 2 teaspoons unflavored powdered gelatin
3 cups heavy cream
1 cup whole milk
¼ cup used coffee grounds
¼ cup sugar
2 pinches kosher salt
Crumbs from Coffee Grounds Biscotti (page 221),
   optional for serving
Apple Scrap Vinegar (page 96),
   optional for serving

If using gelatin sheets, soften them in a small bowl of cold water for 1 minute; squeeze out excess water. If using powdered gelatin, combine with 1 cup warm water and stir until dissolved.

In a small pot, combine the cream, milk, coffee grounds, sugar, and salt. Bring to a simmer and cook, stirring frequently so the milk doesn't scorch at the bottom. Gently stir in the sheet gelatin (make sure there is no water in it) or the powdered gelatin dissolved in the warm water. Once incorporated, remove from the heat, cover, and let the mixture steep for 15 to 20 minutes. Strain.

Divide the panna cotta mixture evenly among 4 small serving bowls and refrigerate for 1 hour until set.

To serve, top each panna cotta with biscotti crumbs and a dash of apple scrap vinegar.

**MAKES 4 SERVINGS / ACTIVE TIME: 15 MIN /
TOTAL TIME: 1 HR 30 MIN**

COFFEE GROUNDS BISCOTTI

2¼ cups all-purpose flour
1½ cups sugar
¼ cup used coffee grounds
2 teaspoons cocoa powder
2 teaspoons baking powder
2 teaspoons kosher salt
2 eggs plus 1 egg yolk
1¼ cups chopped toasted hazelnuts

Position a rack in the middle of the oven and preheat the oven to 350°F. Line two baking sheets with parchment paper.

In a large mixing bowl, mix the flour, sugar, coffee grounds, cocoa powder, baking powder, and salt together. Stir in the eggs and yolk until just incorporated. Fold in the hazelnuts and knead for about 2 minutes, until well incorporated.

Form the dough into 4 logs about 6 inches long and 1½ inches wide. Place on a baking sheet and bake for 20 minutes, until lightly browned.

Let the logs cool. Reduce the oven temperature to 200°F. Cut each log into about 5 to 6 slices, each 6 inches long by ¼-inch-wide. Spread them flat on two baking sheets and bake for an additional 35 to 45 minutes, until hard.

Remove from the oven and cool. Store in an airtight container away from light for up to 15 days.

MAKES ABOUT 20–24 BISCOTTI /
ACTIVE TIME: 30 MIN /
INACTIVE TIME: 1 HR

COFFEE GROUNDS ICE CREAM

2 cups whole milk
2 cups whipping cream
3 tablespoons used coffee grounds
8 egg yolks
1 cup sugar

In a medium saucepan, combine the milk, cream, and coffee grounds and cook over medium high heat until hot and steamy. Remove from the heat, cover with a lid, and let stand for 10 minutes to infuse the flavors.

In a medium bowl, whisk the yolks and sugar while slowly adding the coffee mixture. Pour the combined mixture back into the pan. Cook over medium heat, stirring continuously, until the liquid on the sides of the pot is thickened and coats the back of a wooden spoon, about 7 minutes. Remove from the heat, strain through a fine strainer, and cool.

Freeze in an ice cream maker according to the manufacturer's instructions.

MAKES 2 PINTS /
ACTIVE TIME: 30 MIN /
TOTAL TIME: 2 HRS or more (depending on the ice cream maker)

COFFEE-GROUND-AND-SALT-BAKED SUNCHOKES

The sweetly nutty flavor of sunchokes goes exceptionally well with the burnt, bitter notes of coffee grounds. Salt baking breaks down the toughness of root vegetables. I also make this with old parsnips.

3 pounds coarse salt (see Note)
2 cups used coffee grounds
¼ cup water
2½ pounds (6 cups) sunchokes (Jerusalem artichokes), skin on

Preheat the oven to 400°F. Line an 8 ×11-inch baking sheet with foil.

In a large bowl, stir together the salt, coffee grounds, and water until the consistency of wet sand.

Spread 2 cups of the salt mixture in a ½-inch layer on the baking sheet, creating a bed for the sunchokes. Top with the sunchokes, then cover with the remaining salt mixture, patting it lightly into a mound.

Bake for 1 hour, or until a crust forms. Remove from the oven and let stand 10 minutes. Crack the crust and brush the salt mixture from the vegetables. Serve as a side as you would potatoes.

NOTE:

Coarse kosher salt can be purchased more cheaply in bulk at specialty stores.

SERVES 4 / ACTIVE TIME: 10 MIN /
INACTIVE TIME: 1 HR

BEER

BEER COMES FROM HARDY GRAINS like barley that can survive freezing temperatures. The fizziness of beer is from the fermentation of the grain, and the hops (or other herb) act as a preservative and flavoring. Beer will continue to age in an unopened bottle, affecting its flavor after a few months, depending on the type of beer, and eventually become "flat" with no bubbles. Once a beer bottle is opened, it becomes flat after a day or less.

With the boom of craft breweries, there are so many delicious nuances in beer now. I started using beer for its flavor (and not the fizz) in cooking when we discovered a keg of flat beer at the restaurant.

FLAT BEER JELLY

Use any leftover beer to make this slightly sour jelly. It is a great topping for the Wheat Bran Ice Cream (page 157).

2 cups leftover flat beer
1 cup sugar
1 (3-ounce) box pectin

Simmer the beer in a medium saucepan over medium high heat until reduced to 1 cup, about 15 minutes.

Add the sugar and increase heat to high. In a 1-cup measure, whisk the pectin with one ladle of the hot beer until thoroughly combined. Pour back into the boiling beer jelly and boil for another 2 minutes. Remove from the heat and pour into heat-proof jars. For more information on canning and non-fruit jams see the Resources on page 272.

**MAKES 1½ CUPS / ACTIVE TIME: 5 MIN /
INACTIVE TIME: 20 MIN**

TESTER'S NOTE:
I never thought to make jelly out of beer-can dregs! It had a savory sweet flavor with slightly sour notes. It was great spread on toast or with fine herbs.

TEA

ASIDE FROM WATER, TEA is the most consumed beverage in the world. Teas are mostly made from the leaves of shrubs and herbs, but fruits, berries, and bark can also be brewed into tea. We prefer whole leaf tea to tea bags, but if using tea bags, you can conserve them by steeping them in a pot or by using one bag to make several cups. You can also use them to flavor drinks.

TEA FROM SCRAPS

I LOVE TO BUY single dried herbs and make my own tea blends at home, depending on my mood, my state of health, and the season. Whole leaf teas are incredibly easy to make. Or you can combine whole scraps of dried herb, fruit rinds, and spices. Store your tea blend in an airtight container in a cool, dark space.

To brew, place a scoop in a fine mesh strainer (tea ball or scoop) over the top of a teapot.

In a small pot, bring 2 cups of non-chlorinated spring water to just under a boil.

Remove from the heat and pour over the tea herbs, and steep the ingredients in hot water for 5 to 10 minutes, depending on how strong you prefer your tea. Add honey if you prefer a sweeter tea.

For a **CHRISTMAS TEA**, I like to use dried orange, grapefruit, lemon, and lime peels with allspice, licorice root, cloves, a pinch of dried thyme, dried vanilla bean, a sprig of spruce, and a sprig of dried rosemary.

To make a **SPRING TONIC TEA**, I combine dried rhubarb peel, nettle, mint stems, dried juniper berries, lemon verbena, and lemon thyme.

When it's warm out, I make **SUMMERTIME FLOWERS AND BERRIES TEA**: dried and overripe berries, leaves, and flowers.

CHAMOMILE OLD FASHIONED

The flavor of the chamomile slides in at the end of a sip of this cocktail: a soothing floral herb.

2 ounces (¼ cup) Chamomile Whiskey (below)
⅛ ounce Simple Syrup (below)
1 dash Angostura bitters
Ice
1 strip orange zest

In a pint mixing glass, combine the chamomile whiskey, simple syrup, and bitters. Fill the glass with ice and stir for 45 seconds to 1 minute, until diluted. Add additional ice to an old-fashioned glass. Strain the cocktail into the glass. Express the orange zest and insert over glass.

**MAKES 1 COCKTAIL / ACTIVE TIME: 10 MIN /
TOTAL TIME: 3 HRS**

CHAMOMILE WHISKEY

2 used chamomile tea bags
2 cups rye whiskey

In a glass mason jar, steep the chamomile in the whiskey for 3 hours (or longer if you desire a stronger chamomile flavor). Strain. Store in a cool dark place in a mason jar for 6 months.

**MAKES 2 CUPS, enough for 8 cocktails /
ACTIVE TIME: 5 MIN / TOTAL TIME: 3 HRS or longer**

SIMPLE SYRUP

1 cup demerara brown sugar
¾ cup water

In a small pan, combine the sugar and water and heat for 5 minutes, until the sugar is dissolved. Remove from heat and store in the fridge for up to 2 weeks.

MAKES 1½ CUPS / TIME: 10 MIN

Other Ways to Enjoy Old Tea and Tea Bags

A single tea bag can be reused on the spot for several cups of tea. Brewed tea should last for 5 days in the refrigerator and 6 to 8 months in the freezer.

If you are a daily tea drinker, collect the used bags and store them in a Ziploc bag in the refrigerator. When you have a handful, steep them in a jug of water in the refrigerator. Add two used lemon halves and some honey (from the bottom of the honey jar) for iced tea.

Steep 5 used green tea bags in ½ cup milk and add to standard yellow or vanilla cake recipe.

Tea can be used for poaching fish, chicken, or rice to impart the tea flavor. Steep ½ cup used green tea leaves in 6 cups hot water for 3 minutes. Use this water as the base for your poaching liquid and add other seasonings such as ginger, lime, or lemongrass.

9

LEFTOVERS

LEFTOVERS USUALLY MEANS some uneaten or partially eaten food left on a plate after a meal. Before refrigeration, creating dishes from leftover food scraps was a common practice in every culture. But today, rather than being considered a creative frugality, leftovers get a bad rap: from the boredom of repetition to the stigma of serving them to anyone but yourself (certainly not guests) to the bother of having to figure out how to use them to concerns about freshness. (To learn more about safety and leftovers, see below.)

In this chapter you'll find a host of strategies for creating inventive and delicious meals from what you already have in your refrigerator.

Leftovers & Safety

When in doubt, follow these recommendations from the USDA.

- Leftovers should be refrigerated within 2 hours of cooking. If the temperature is 90°F or over (as at a summer picnic), the food will safely keep for only 1 hour before it has to be refrigerated.

- Cold foods like deli platters should be kept at 40°F or below.

- When refrigerating or freezing leftover hot soup, it can be brought to a cooler temperature quickly by dividing it into smaller containers.

- Leftovers can be kept safely in the refrigerator for 3 to 4 days, after which the risk of food poisoning increases. If there is a good chance the leftovers will not be used in that time, it is best to freeze them immediately, where they will keep 3 to 4 months. To prevent loss of moisture/freezer burn, wrap tightly in plastic wrap and then foil.

- To thaw, keep in a leak-proof plastic bag and thaw in the refrigerator or, less preferably, immersed in cold water or zap in a microwave.

- Soups and stews can be directly heated from the freezer without first thawing.

SOUPS, STOCKS, & BROTHS

THE UNIVERSAL MELTING POT for scraps and leftovers is stock or broth. Although the words are often used interchangeably, a *stock* is usually made from bones, is thick, and has a deep, rich flavor; it forms the base of many an excellent sauce. A *broth* is thinner and uses more meat as the base and so is generally less rich than stock. *Soup* contains other elements, such as grains (noodles, rice, barley), vegetables, and sometimes chunks of meat scraps—and is a dish or meal in itself.

VEGETABLE SCRAP & PEEL STOCK

This "no bones" vegetable-based stock derives its richness instead from the briny flavors of konbu and the smokiness of charring the vegetables first. Use the fast-char method with whatever vegetable scraps you would otherwise throw out, such as celeriac skin, corn husks, onion skins, celery, carrot peels, parsnip peels, and mushroom stems.

MAKES A LARGE POTFUL ABOUT 3 QUARTS but will depend on how much scraps you have, the more the merrier

ACTIVE TIME: 30 MIN

TOTAL TIME: OVERNIGHT, PLUS 8 HRS. This is a great opportunity to use a slow cooker; then you can just set the cooker to a low setting

1 sheet konbu
5 to 10 cups vegetable scraps, such as onions, root vegetables, cauliflower cores
1 to 2 cups aromatics, such as parsley or rosemary stems

Make a light konbu dashi by steeping the konbu in 4 cups warm water overnight. Remove the konbu and store the dashi in the refrigerator for up to 3 months.

On a grill, or in a dry (no oil) cast iron skillet over high heat, lightly char the vegetable scraps for a minute or less, until just blackened on the edges.

In a large heavy pot or slow cooker, combine the charred vegetable scraps, aromatics, 4 cups dashi, and 2 cups water. Simmer over low heat or in a slow cooker on medium for 5 to 7 hours, until very tender and stock is cloudy. The stock can be frozen as is without straining.

On Chicken Stock

Real homemade stock cannot be compared to the stock or broth sold in cans and boxes. Real stock is what is reduced by chefs into sauce to create a complex richness of flavor. Use the chicken bones and cartilage, including the feet, neck, and back bones. For a clear stock, the bones of the chicken should be rinsed in clear water first before adding, to remove any impurities that will cloud the stock. Meat-based stock also requires skimming off the foam.

On Bone Broth

Of course broth made with bones is nothing new, but recently it has gotten a boost from high-profile athletes extolling its health benefits, particularly the cartilage. The main difference between bone broth and many a chicken broth is that bone broth commonly adds ¼ cup vinegar for a 4-quart batch of broth and the bones are cooked much longer.

On Slow Cookers

A lot of the reason that scraps are thrown away is because they are hard or fibrous. This is why a slow cooker is one of the best ways to use scraps. I throw a lot of things in the slow cooker—like whole cele-riac—and they come out beautifully. Not only is it ideal for making a tender stew, but it's also great for cooking beans, steel-cut oats, and a variety of other ingredients.

NINE EVERYDAY MEALS, ENDLESS POSSIBILITIES

ONE OF THE GREATEST OBSTACLES to cooking at home is the boredom of eating the same things over and over. Meat and potatoes, soup and salad, spaghetti and meatballs. The fun thing about cooking with scraps is that it can be a little different every time, depending what you have. The key is to have versatile recipes up your sleeve. The following nine dishes, inspired by global food traditions, will help keep dinner interesting.

Typically, cookbook recipes are very specific about what ingredients and quantities are required. If one ingredient is missing or you don't have the exact amount the recipe calls for, a special trip to the supermarket is required, leading to more leftovers and a vicious cycle. Instead of being so rigid, we think the key to making plenty is versatility. So if you only know nine recipes, but they are infinitely flexible, then you are well on your way to interesting dinners every night.

These basic dishes can be prepared on weekdays, lazy nights, or when you are just hungry and want to scrounge up something to eat other than a cracker or takeout. (Tip: When serving, don't call it "leftovers" and it will already seem more delicious.)

Each recipe has two ingredient sections: The first is the basic necessary ingredients (many of which are found in the list of core pantry items at right). The second is a longer list of suggested scraps and leftovers, from which you can pick and choose your ingredients, based on preference and what's available. Or use the scraps list as a guide for using what's in your refrigerator. Each cooking method is simple and each recipe can be a one-dish meal.

16
PANTRY FUNDAMENTALS

Stock your pantry with the following base ingredients; then it will be easy to add scraps to cook any of the meals that follow.

Oil: olive oil, a neutral oil (grapeseed or sunflower oil), sesame oil

Salt: sea, kosher, or Maldon

Soy sauce or tamari sauce

Rice (jasmine, basmati, Thai)

Eggs, organic and free-range

Flour

Milk, organic, and cream

Butter, organic, unsalted

Vinegar, rice, red wine, apple cider (see Resources on page 272 for more on vinegars)

Yogurt

Pasta (wheat based and rice based)

Ginger

Green onions or shallots

Lemon!

Whole peppercorns, chili sauce, sriracha

Cheeses (for grating, filling)

1

OMELET OR FRITTATA

Definitions of omelet versus frittata vary. An omelet is generally folded over the filling and is supposed to be fluffy, whereas a frittata is cut like a pie, can feed a group well, and is—many times, but not always—finished in the oven. Use whatever method you feel comfortable with and have time for, and don't worry about what you call it!

Essential Ingredients
Neutral vegetable oil, such as grapeseed, for sautéing
1 tablespoon unsalted butter
5 large eggs
Salt and pepper

Scraps and Leftovers
1 or 2 cooked potatoes (if boiled or baked, cut into 1-inch dice)
Meat scraps (bits of bacon, shredded chicken, or ham)
¼ cup cooked greens and raw herbs (parsley, dill, chives, or tarragon), finely chopped

Start with the scraps and leftovers: Heat the oil in a 10-inch pan over medium heat. Add the potatoes and/or meat and sauté until lightly browned. Remove from the pan.

In the same 10-inch pan, melt the butter over low heat. Pour the eggs into the pan and whisk briefly so the whites and yolks are mixed. Add the greens and herbs, and the meat and/or potatoes and cook for a minute, until the eggs are set on the bottom and still look liquidy on the top. With a spatula, flip the mixture on its other side and remove from heat. Let sit for a minute, until set, and serve.

SERVES 2 / TIME: 15 MIN

2

QUICHE

This savory pie, French in origin, is delicious with a wide range of meats, vegetables, mushrooms, and cheeses. P.S.: Quiche also makes a great leftover (of leftovers!).

Essential Ingredients
1 store-bought shell of piecrust dough (or use your favorite homemade dough)
3 eggs
2 cups half-and-half
Pinch nutmeg
Salt and pepper
Pinch cayenne pepper
1 tablespoon butter

Scraps and Leftovers
Chopped onion
Bacon or ham
Broccoli or spinach, chopped
Mushrooms
1 cup assorted grated flavorful hard cheeses (Gruyère, Swiss, Cheddar, Parmesan)

Preheat the oven to 425°F. Bake the pie shell for 12 minutes, until the edges just start to brown lightly.

In a medium bowl, whisk together the eggs, half-and-half, nutmeg, salt, and pepper and set aside.

Meanwhile, in a large saucepan or skillet, melt the butter over low heat. Add the onion and bacon or other meat and cook at medium heat, roughly breaking up the meat with a wooden spoon, until the onion is tender and the meat is cooked. Remove from the pan.

Add the broccoli or spinach to the pan and cook until spinach is just wilted or the broccoli is turning brighter green, that is, not fully cooked. Fill the pie shell with the cooked scraps and leftovers and the mushrooms and cheese. Pour the egg mixture over the top. Bake for 30 minutes, until the top is melted and set.

SERVES 4 / ACTIVE TIME: 30 MIN / INACTIVE TIME: 30 MIN

3

SAVORY PANCAKES

Savory pancakes, or *okonomiyaki,* are a popular comfort food in Japan. In fact, *okonomi* means "what you wish" and *yaki* is "to grill." As evidenced by the name, the ingredients are very flexible; different regions as well as individual families have their own preferred versions. This recipe is for a flour pancake with some eggs, filled with favorite leftovers. (If your dining partner hates seafood, keep it for your pancake and give him or her more vegetables.) I like to serve it with a thick hoisin or oyster-style sauce, Sriracha, and pickles. You could also serve the pancakes with the Overripe Pear Barbecue Sauce (page 123) or the Spicy Beet Chili Sauce (page 25).

If you decide you really like this dish, you can get fanatical and buy special okonomiyaki flour online, as well as okonomi sauce. You can also substitute dashi stock for the water to enhance the flavor.

Essential Ingredients
1 cup all-purpose flour
⅔ cup water
4 or more eggs
2 tablespoons neutral oil

Scraps and Leftovers
3 cups shredded cabbage*
¼ cup chopped or shredded seafood (shrimp, crab, or squid)*
¼ cup chopped green onions*
¼ cup grated potato
¼ cup chopped green vegetable

* Although flexible, these are the most commonly used ingredients in okonomiyaki.

In a large bowl, whisk the flour with the water and eggs until it has the consistency of a thin batter. Heat the oil in a large cast iron skillet or griddle until very hot. Ladle 2 portions of batter onto the griddle to make 2 or more pancakes. Divide the scraps and leftovers into portions and use to top each pancake. Cook for 3 minutes, until bubbles form on the top of the batter and the bottoms are browned. Flip and cook for another minute, until no longer liquidy.

SERVES 2 / TIME: 15 MIN

4

RICE SALAD

Indian and Middle Eastern cuisines feature a lot of composed rice dishes. Especially inspiring are the multi-grain salads of Yotam Ottolenghi in his book *Plenty More*, from which this recipe is adapted. There are a myriad of combinations that mix rices, quinoa, and barley with seafood, meat, vegetables, and herbs. These reflect the preferences for and availability of different foods in different regions of the world, as well as techniques for the rice itself, whether fluffy or sticky; baked, steamed, or boiled. If you have a favorite rice salad, master it and then get creative with using the things you have on hand. The salads are delicious and, since they don't use heavy dressings, can last the entire week packed in lunch boxes or as leftovers of leftovers.

Essential Ingredients
3 cups basmati rice and/or grains (quinoa, wild rice, etc.)
¼ cup olive oil
Grated zest and juice of 1 lemon
Salt and pepper

Scraps and Leftovers
¾ cup nuts (slivered almonds, walnuts, pecans, pine nuts) or seeds
1 cup dried tangy fruits (raisins, currants, dried sour cherries, and/or dried cranberries)
2 cups fresh herbs (parsley, tarragon, and/or basil with smaller amounts of mint), chopped

Cook the rices and grains separately, according to their respective package instructions. Drain and let cool.

In a very large serving bowl, combine the rices and grains with the scraps and leftovers. Add the olive oil, lemon zest, and juice and toss. Finish with salt and pepper to taste.

SERVES 4 / TIME: 45 MIN

See also pages 151–152 for more ways to use rice.

5

PASTA

Pasta has come a long way from spaghetti and meatballs. Today, both chefs and home cooks look at pasta as a blank slate for whatever is in season and tasty.

Essential Ingredients
Salt
8 ounces pasta
Olive oil

Scraps and Leftovers
Dark leafy vegetables
Chopped onion
Mushroom stems
Meat scraps
Herb scraps (thyme and oregano, etc.), finely chopped
Nuts
Grated lemon zest
Pesto (see pages 51, 58, and 60)
Grated Parmesan cheese
Cracked black pepper

Bring a large pot of salted water to a boil. Add the pasta and cook according to package instructions. Drain, transfer to a large bowl, and keep warm.

Meanwhile, in a large pan, heat the olive oil and sauté the greens, onion, mushroom stems, and meat scraps until tender. Transfer to the bowl with the pasta and toss in the chopped herb scraps and nuts. Serve with lemon zest, pesto, grated Parmesan, and cracked pepper.

SERVES 4 / TIME: 30 MIN

6

ASIAN STYLE NOODLES

This home-style way of cooking noodles is not what you normally find in Asian restaurants (that is, fried or very sauced). Instead it uses lots of ginger, and incorporates vinegar and Sriracha as condiments. Gluten-free Asian rice or bean thread noodles work well, but it is also is fine with any shaped wheat pasta.

Essential Ingredients

8–10 ounces noodles or pasta (any type of pasta will do, even mixing different noodles left in boxes, as long as they take the same cooking time)

2 tablespoons sesame oil

Chopped onion (optional)

1 tablespoon sliced or finely diced fresh ginger

Minced garlic (optional)

1 tablespoon soy sauce

Apple cider vinegar or rice vinegar

Sriracha sauce

Scraps and Leftovers

Leftover meat (hamburger, cooked chicken, bacon strips, or ham)

Greens (broccoli, cauliflower, cabbage, and/or spinach), chopped

Carrots, cut into matchsticks (optional)

Asian herbs (chives, coriander, and/or Thai basil), chopped

Bring a large pot of salted water to a boil and cook the pasta according to package instructions until al dente. Drain.

Meanwhile, in a large saucepan or cast iron skillet, heat the sesame oil over medium heat. Add the onion, ginger, garlic (if using), and any uncooked meat. Cook, stirring, for 5 minutes, until browned. Add the soy sauce, chopped greens, available carrots and herbs, and sauté. If you have a large enough skillet or wok, add the cooked noodles to the pan and toss so the pasta soaks up some of the brown bits and oils from the bottom of the pan. Otherwise remove from heat and combine with the pasta in a large bowl. Serve with additional soy sauce, vinegar, and Sriracha to taste.

SERVES 4 / TIME: 30 MIN

RESTAURANT LEFTOVERS: TO **TAKE** OR **NOT** TO TAKE

WHAT ABOUT LEFTOVERS FROM DINING OUT?
When eating out it is more difficult to control portion size, often resulting in uneaten food. But the very name *doggy bag* implies that we don't want to admit that humans are actually eating the leftovers we bring home from restaurants. There is no reason why, particularly if the diner requests it, a dining establishment should frown on or not permit packing and taking home the remains of a thoroughly enjoyed meal.

Of course there are certain types of cuisine that are better suited to take home and give the leftover treatment. This may also be instructive for home cooks seeking to make the most of home-cooked meals.

TAKE-HOME DO'S:

- Curries (Indian, Thai, Vietnamese), which can be frozen and reheated
- Braised dishes such as stews
- Chinese food
- Desserts
- Soups
- Steak and chops
- Cheese and charcuterie plates
- Pizza (It's interesting that of all the leftover meals, no one seems to have a problem with pizza. It is the most consumed leftover food in the United States despite the cold, hardened cheese and chewy leftover bread crusts.)

TAKE-HOME DON'TS:

- Raw fish
- Raw shellfish such as oysters
- Salads with creamy dressing (unless the dressing is on the side)

7

TACOS OR QUESADILLAS

Enjoy any number of fillings wrapped in or sandwiched between flour-based tortillas.

Essential Ingredients
4 or 8 tortillas (corn for tacos, flour for quesadillas)
Olive oil (for quesadillas)
Grated cheese (for quesadillas)

Scraps and Leftovers
Cooked meats (chicken or shredded pork) or cooked fish
Kale or other vegetable tops, chopped
Cabbage cores, shredded
Onion scraps, minced
Herb scraps, chopped
Pickled radish
Coriander seeds
Pesto (see pages 51, 58, and 60) and/or salsa verde (page 51)
Shredded lettuce (page 75)

For tacos: Stuff the tortillas with the leftovers and scraps and add something spicy.

    For quesadillas: Heat 1 teaspoon olive oil in a cast iron skillet over medium high heat. Add one tortilla and then quickly add a layer of the scraps and leftovers of choice, with at least ½ cup grated cheese. Top with another tortilla and flip with a wide spatula, browning lightly on both sides until the cheese melts out the sides. Repeat to make 4 quesadillas.

SERVES 4 / TIME: 30 MIN

S

STEW

Odd-lot and leftover ingredients can make a hearty stew. If you freeze the gravy, browned bits, and some large chunks of meat from a roast, they can be used as the starter for a stew.

Essential Ingredients
2 tablespoons olive oil
Chopped onion
2 tablespoons unsalted butter
2 cups stock (can include leftover meats)
2 tablespoons Worcestershire sauce
3 tablespoons all-purpose flour
Salt and pepper

Scraps and Leftovers
Vegetable scraps (celery leaves, mushy tomatoes, ugly potato chunks, unpeeled root vegetable ends, chunks of daikon radish, carrots, and/or shriveled mushrooms)
Mushy tomatoes
Leftover cooked meat (bacon or ham, chunks of bone-in meat or pork shoulder)
Leftover wine (2 cups is great)
Whole herbs (thyme, oregano, basil)

Preheat the oven to 300°F. Over a stove, using a Le Creuset pot or Dutch oven, heat the oil and sauté the onion for 5 minutes, until lightly browned. Add the butter, vegetable scraps, tomatoes, and meat bits and sauté until lightly browned. Add the stock, wine, Worcestershire sauce, and herbs. In a measuring cup, whisk flour into a few tablespoons of the liquid, then add to stew for thickening. Cover and bake for 2 hours at a simmer (reduce the oven temperature if it begins boiling). Add salt and pepper, to taste.

SERVES 2–4 PERSONS as a supper; can be made more filling for a dinner if you serve with crusty bread and cheese and a salad
ACTIVE TIME: 30 MIN / TOTAL TIME: 2 HRS 30 MIN

9

HOT POT

A hot pot meal is a great vehicle for leftover scraps. Family and friends gather 'round a table with the hot pot in the center. At home this is usually a tabletop gas stove (not a camping stove; see Resources, page 272). Hot pot aficionados might use a dual "yin yang" steel hot pot, with two separated compartments; one side can be spicy and the other bland, or one side can be meat-based and the other vegetarian. You can just use a shallow large pan over the stove, although you miss some of the communal atmosphere. Food is cooked as you go, and everyone serves themselves, so there can be as much or little as is desired.

Essential Ingredients

Water or broth

Dipping sauces (chili bean paste, tamari sauce, and sesame oil with chopped green onions; or ponzu sauce with grated daikon radish and chopped green onions)

Cooked rice

Asian-style pickles (crunchy vinegared radish peels on page 89, or other rice vinegar–based pickle)

Scraps and Leftovers

Root vegetables (carrots, radishes), cut into 2-inch chunks

Corn cobs, with or without the kernels

Thinly sliced uncooked meat (chicken, pork, beef, including innards such as tripe, tongue, kidney)

Squash, peeled of outermost fibrous skin and cut into 2-inch chunks

Cabbage family vegetables, roughly chopped into 3-inch chunks

Mushrooms, of mixed varieties

Firm tofu, cut into 1- to 2-inch cubes

Fill a large pot with water or broth, adding any optional root vegetables and corn cobs, as well as any vegetable ends and meat bones you have on hand. Simmer, skimming off the foam, for about 30 minutes, then remove any ends and bones so that diners don't get confused with the dipping ingredients. Alternatively, if you prefer a stronger flavored liquid, add one of the dashis; for a spicier broth, add chili bean paste.

Meanwhile, arrange the leftover meat on one platter and the leftover vegetables and tofu on another platter. Prepare the dipping sauces.

Reduce the heat to medium and have guests add the meat, vegetables, and tofu to the water, starting first with those that take longer to cook. Skim off any foam from the surface of the water.

As each ingredient is done, dip in the dipping sauce of choice and serve with hot steamed rice and pickles.

SERVES 2 TO 8, as many people as can fit around the pot / TIME: 30 MIN to whenever everyone is full

LEFTOVER PASTA

CERTAIN meals taste even better the day after, like beef stew and roasts, croquettes and patties, composed rice salads, lasagna, and curries. But did you know some can actually be healthier the next day? Pasta may be less fattening once reheated, according to the BBC. Studies have found that cooking, cooling, and reheating pasta (i.e., the leftover "method") inhibited blood glucose (sugar) spikes by 50 percent, so that the pasta functioned more like a fiber, a resistant starch.

Since it's often difficult to judge how much pasta to prepare, invariably people are going to end up with leftovers, whether cooked in a dish or plain.

SOME IDEAS FOR LEFTOVER PASTA:

- **Supplement a satisfying soup or stew:** Add leftover pasta in the last 5 minutes before serving, long enough to cook the pasta but still retain its texture.

- **Make an Italian-style frittata:** Combine 2 cups cooked spaghetti or other pasta, 2 eggs, and ¼ cup grated Parmesan or other hard cheese. In a medium pan, heat 1 tablespoon olive oil and 1 tablespoon unsalted butter. Add the pasta mixture, along with any bits of sausage, bacon, or veggies you might have on hand. Press down with the back of a spatula so it forms a cake-like shape. Cook for 5 minutes, until golden brown. Flip and fry on the other side for 1 minute, until it too is golden brown. Cut into wedges and serve.

- **Compose a pasta salad:** Combine cooked shells or penne-type pasta with an olive oil vinaigrette, crunchy diced vegetables and scraps (such as celery and celery leaves), and lots of herbs.

- **Make a crunchy casserole:** Place leftover pasta in a 3-quart casserole dish. Add meat (canned tuna, shredded chicken, ham), chopped crunchy and green vegetables (celery, red pepper, mushrooms), and a cream sauce. Most important: Top with crushed seeds/crackers and lots of tangy grated cheese (leftover ends and rinds are fine!). Bake at 425°F for 1 hour, until the cheese has melted and is charred and crispy.

- **Crisp it on the stovetop:** Heat a griddle pan or cast iron skillet over high heat, throw in some leftover pasta, and cook until sizzling. Flip once one side is crisp and dark brown. Grate cheese or other condiment on top.

10

FORGOTTEN FOOD: FORAGING

Humanity has foraged for food since before the advent of agriculture.

TODAY, MANY CULTURES around the globe still keep the old traditions alive, even though they may no longer need to eat wild foods to survive. In Scandinavia, it is a common practice in the long summer days for most everyone to fill baskets with berries, mushrooms, wild herbs, and sea plants. Meanwhile, here in the United States, wild mushroom collecting is so popular that in order to prevent overharvesting it is often regulated by local and state governments. But you needn't go to state forests (foraging may be illegal in some states) to find the weeds that may be in your backyard. There can be a little bit of wild almost anywhere, overlooked and "wasted."

When NOMA wanted to make a true local and seasonal cuisine, we started looking at everyday things around us. We didn't stop at the farms.

We saw the forest, we saw the sea. Frankly, I was thinking, *How the f* is there going to be enough fresh food to get from there in the dead of winter?* But yes: You can put a forest on the plate. It's delicious. It's good for you.

Edible meadow of *Rudbeckia laciniata*, a favored green of the Cherokee.

EVERGREENS

EVERGREENS HAVE LONG BEEN a food and medicine source for indigenous peoples. Native Americans extensively used the white pine, spruce, and fir inner bark, needles, young tips, branches, and pitch for tea and gum.

When I came to the United States, I couldn't believe how many Norway spruce trees there were. I saw that not only were there evergreen trees in forests, but they are planted all over the country as part of the landscape design. Of course, people also buy firs, pines, and spruces as Christmas trees—putting lights on them, enjoying them at Christmas, and then throwing them out.

Identification

An evergreen tree, unlike a deciduous tree, does not lose its leaves in the winter. But this does not mean that evergreens are static. New growth appears in the spring, and white pine trees drop their needles in the fall.

Edible evergreens are commonly distinguished first by looking closely at the leaf shape and formation: (a) flat and scale-like leaves found on juniper trees such as the eastern red cedar, *Juniperus virginiana;* or (b) needle-like, single or clustered needles, found on pine, fir, and spruce trees.

Some common evergreen trees are found in the wild in parts of the United States but are also widely planted in backyards across the country:

NORWAY SPRUCE, *Picea abies,* (there are also black, red, and blue spruces): Up to 8 inches long with large cones, the tree itself has strongly drooping branches. The dark green needles are singly borne, and square when you look at a cross section.

WHITE PINE, *Pinus strobus:* The long thin needles are found in clusters, about 5 per bundle.

DOUGLAS FIR, *Psedotsuga menziesii:* The western evergreen has straight flat needles as well as distinctive cones with turned-up bracts.

Safe Collection and Consumption

The needles of varieties of pine, spruce, or fir may be pokey, but they are not poisonous. But be careful not to consume the berry of just any evergreen, some of which are toxic, like the yew.

The main groups of evergreens in the Northern Hemisphere have a long history of edibility and uses. As with any wild foraging, be careful to be sure that you know the history and management of the land on which the tree grows, and that the tree has not been sprayed or injected with oils or pesticides.

Because evergreens are often sold for ornamental use in landscapes, they are bred as different "named" variations and cultivars. Since these cultivars may differ from the straight wild species, the most prudent course would be to stick to the straight or wild species, unless a particular ornamental variety has a documented history of culinary use.

Tree Flavors and Uses

Evergreen trees have an amazing flavor: citrusy and piney. You can almost feel the fresh clean-ness you experience when you walk through pine and spruce and fir forests. It's not that crazy to think of trees as a spice if you know that cinnamon is a bark, and juniper berries are the cone of an evergreen, and maple syrup is the sap from a tree, and capers are the bud of a bush.

YOUNG TIPS

In the spring, evergreen spruce trees sprout baby needles on the ends of last year's branches. Next spring (in May in New York), when you pass by a spruce tree, take a glance at it. You may first see little brown papery casings, which clothe the emerging tips. The casings will split and fall off, and then you can't miss the neon lime green tips, which are soft before they harden into needles. Their sweet, lightly citrusy flavor is addictive: I like to break them apart raw and scatter them like an herb or spice in cucumber salad, rice pilaf, desserts, and soups (see Smoky Potato Scrap Broth, page 84).

It is very easy to make spruce salt. Chop up fresh spruce tips and leave them in salt; and the spruce tips will dry into the salt. Sprinkle instead of just plain salt on a protein, such as lamb, pork, or fish.

As the tips open more and fan out, and before they harden into needles, they become a little sharper in flavor, and are good for an aromatic oil or syrup. Spruce tips also freeze well.

MATURE NEEDLES

We have recipes for sugar, syrup, and powder in this section.

Opposite: Norway spruce tips in the spring.

SPRUCE NEEDLE POWDER

I call this "Eat Your Christmas Tree." Every year in the city I see so many Christmas trees decorated with beautiful lights; then, weeks later, there are so many trees left on the sidewalk to be thrown away in the trash. But you can make this powder and add it to your baked goods. You can also make a sugar with spruce powder: combine in equal amounts (e.g., 2 tablespoons sugar and 2 tablespoons spruce powder) and use to substitute for sugar, for example in a gravlax.

8 12-inch-long boughs (with needles attached) cut from a Norway spruce tree or another evergreen such as Douglas fir (be sure they have not been sprayed; this includes your Christmas tree!)

Use a dehydrator or preheat the oven to 150°F. Spread the boughs out in a single layer on a baking sheet.

Dry in the dehydrator or oven for 7 hours, until the needles snap when bent. Remove the needles from the twigs; they should easily fall off to the touch. If not, then you need to extend the drying time.

In a spice or coffee grinder, starting on low speed and finishing at high speed, grind the needles into a fine powder. The powder will be highly aromatic. Store in an airtight container for up to 6 months.

MAKES ¼ CUP POWDER (1 CUP NEEDLES) / ACTIVE TIME: 40 MIN / TOTAL TIME: 8 HRS

SPRUCE SUGAR COOKIES

4 tablespoons Spruce Needle Powder
½ cup granulated sugar
⅔ cup (1¼ sticks) unsalted butter, softened
2 eggs
½ teaspoon grated lemon zest
2 cups all-purpose flour
2 teaspoons baking powder
½ teaspoon kosher salt
1 tablespoon confectioners' sugar, for dusting

In a food processor, combine 2 tablespoons of the spruce powder and the granulated sugar. Mix in the butter and then add the eggs and lemon zest. Mix in the flour, baking powder, and salt until just combined.

Form the dough into a 2-inch-thick log and wrap tightly in plastic wrap; refrigerate for at least 30 minutes.

Preheat the oven to 350°F. Line a baking sheet with parchment paper.

Remove the dough from the refrigerator and slice into ¼-inch-thick rounds. Place on the baking sheet and bake for 10 minutes, until lightly browned around the edges. Dust with the remaining 2 tablespoons spruce powder and the confectioners' sugar.

MAKES 36 COOKIES / TIME: 1 HR

SPRUCE TREE FLODEBOLLER

Flodeboller is a popular sweet treat in Denmark. Its marzipan wafer base is topped with a fluffy unbaked meringue, then covered with a layer of chocolate. This flodeboller uses a spruce-infused meringue.

Marzipan

1 (7-ounce) tube commercially prepared marzipan, available at supermarkets and online

1–2 tablespoons Spruce Needle Powder (at left)

12 ounces 70 percent dark chocolate, chopped

¼ cup young spruce tips (optional)

Meringue

2 egg whites

2 tablespoons Spruce Needle Syrup (page 254), at room temperature

¾ cup sugar

1 tablespoon corn syrup

¼ cup water

3 tablespoons Spruce Needle Powder (at left), for dusting

For the marzipan: On a parchment-covered flat surface, roll out the marzipan to ¼ inch thick, incorporating the spruce powder liberally while rolling. Using a round cookie cutter, cut out circles. Remove and re-form the unused marzipan into circles. These circles are the marzipan "biscuits" that form the base.

In a medium pot over low heat, melt 7 ounces of the chocolate. Remove from the heat, add the remaining 5 ounces chopped chocolate, and stir until completely melted (this double melting method is important in order to properly set the chocolate).

Dip the marzipan biscuits in the chocolate with a fork and scrape along the side of the pot to remove excess chocolate from the biscuit. Place the chocolate-covered marzipan biscuits on a wire rack. Set aside.

For the meringue: In a mixer, beat the egg whites while gently adding the spruce syrup. Stop mixing as soon as the egg whites begin to get foamy.

In a small pot, combine the sugar, corn syrup, and water; bring to a boil, and boil without stirring for 3 minutes, until the bubbles begin to look larger and the activity begins to slow. Check with a candy thermometer that the temperature just reaches 240°F. Immediately remove the pot from the heat.

Turn the mixer on at medium speed and slowly pour the hot syrup down the side of the mixer bowl into the meringue. Turn the mixer to high speed and whip for 5 minutes, until the bottom of the mixer bowl is room temperature and no longer hot to the touch, and the mixture has become a stiff, glossy meringue. Fold in the spruce powder gently so that the meringue does not deflate.

Place the chocolate-covered marzipans on a wire rack over a baking sheet lined with parchment paper. Transfer the meringue to a piping bag fitted with a large #8 star tip. Pipe the meringue atop the wafers in a vertical cone, resembling a witch's hat or Hershey's kiss, about 2 inches high. Chill until set, about 1 hour.

Warm the rest of the chocolate, and spoon more on top of the chilled meringue until covered.

Chill the flodebollers in the refrigerator for 10 minutes, until the chocolate forms a shell. Sprinkle with the spruce tips or powder.

MAKES 2 DOZEN / TIME: 45 MIN

Clockwise from upper left: Spruce Sugar Cookies, page 250 / Spruce Marshmallows, page 255 / Spruce Tree Flodeboller, page 251

SPRUCE NEEDLE SYRUP

This versatile, piney flavored syrup can be used instead of sugar in iced tea or other drinks, cocktails, and for poaching fruits.

4 (6-inch-long) fresh spruce needles on the branch
1 cup sugar
1 cup water

Crack and bend the spruce branches or hit them with the back of a knife to release some of the oils. In a small pot, bring the sugar, water, and spruce sprigs to a boil. Reduce the heat to medium and simmer for a few minutes, until the sugar is dissolved. Reduce the heat and simmer for another 5 minutes. Turn the heat off and let stand for 30 minutes, to infuse the flavor of the spruce more fully. Strain and store in an airtight jar in the refrigerator for up to a week.

MAKES 1½ CUPS / TIME: 40 MIN

SPRUCE MARSHMALLOWS

Roast the marshmallows over an open flame, sprinkling liberally with additional spruce powder after roasting. The homemade marshmallows will keep in the fridge, covered, overnight, or at room temperature in a sealed container for 2 days.

2¼ cups granulated sugar
1 cup water
½ tablespoon corn syrup
12 sheets gelatin, softened
1 tablespoon plus ½ cup Spruce Needle Powder (page 250), plus more for dusting
¼ cup confectioners' sugar for the baking sheet and ¼ cup for dusting

In a medium pot, bring the granulated sugar, ½ cup water, and corn syrup to a boil and cook until the bubbling slows (240°F on a candy thermometer, if you have one).

Meanwhile, in a mixer bowl, mix the gelatin, the remaining ½ cup water, and the 1 tablespoon spruce powder. Turn the mixer to medium-high and pour the sugar syrup down the side of the bowl. Then increase the mixer speed to high and beat until stiff like a marshmallow. Let the bowl cool.

Gradually fold in the ½ cup spruce powder.

Dust a large (12 × 18-inch) baking sheet with confectioners' sugar to prevent sticking. Spread the marshmallow mixture evenly across the sheet (or pipe it on the sheet in even rows using a piping bag with an Ateco #808 or Wilton 1A tip). Top with more sugar and chill for 1 hour.

Cut the marshmallow into 2-inch squares. Toss in equal parts spruce powder and confectioners' sugar.

MAKES ABOUT 50 / TIME: 15 MIN

NUTS, FRUITS, FLOWERS, & HERBS (WEEDS)

NUTS, FRUITS, FLOWERS, AND HERBS (WEEDS) are the kinds of food I get really excited about. They make a dish come alive. Here is what I mean.

Tree flavors: Many parts of the tree are edible, including roots, leaves, bark, and the inner water. I love tree water, which is the inner sap before it is boiled down to syrup; it has more flavor (and nutrients) than the sugar you buy in the store. We use a lot of birch in various places in the Northern Hemisphere, but you also have maple here in North America. Of course most people are familiar with tree nuts, but you may not appreciate how special fresh tree nuts are, because you can buy them stored, shelled, and roasted anywhere. True fresh nuts have a light, fresh, juicy flavor.

Black Walnuts

Black walnut trees are indigenous to the United States. Their wood is prized as one of the hardest in the forest. The nuts of the black walnut have a green hull when they first fall off the tree. If you touch the green hull, it can permanently stain. So to get to the nut inside, the hull must be removed with gloves; or, alternatively, leave the green "balls" outside and eventually the green outer husk will fall off. The inner shell can then be rinsed and stored.

To crack, soak the dry shells in water for 2 hours and then keep them covered and moist overnight. Crack on a stone base (not wood) with a small mallet or hammer and pick the nuts out with a nutpick. The nuts should be smooth and milky with a brown skin.

BLACK WALNUT PUREE

Black walnuts have a richer flavor than the English walnuts sold in the store. They can be used as a dessert flavoring in whipped cream, as a mousse, or a mixed savory as a yogurt sauce or spread.

2 cups black walnuts, shelled

2 cups konbu dashi (see first step of Vegetable Scrap & Peel Stock, page 230)

¼ cup brown sugar

¼ vanilla bean, halved and scraped

2 tablespoons walnut oil

2 teaspoons white wine vinegar

¼ teaspoon kosher salt

In a medium pot over medium heat, cook the walnuts, dashi, brown sugar, and vanilla until the nuts soften, about 20 minutes (the nuts may be quite variable, so this time is only a rough estimate).

Transfer the nuts and liquid to a blender and add the oil, vinegar, and salt. Blend until smooth. Store in a glass jar in the refrigerator for up to 2 weeks.

MAKES 1 CUP / TIME: 20 MIN

TREE
BARK

BARK ADDS GREAT flavor in grilling or roasting (think of hickory chips). But be careful with the use of bark because stripping a tree of bark all around will kill the tree by "girdling" it. Some barks you have here, like shagbark hickory bark (*Carya ovata*), will naturally exfoliate. Also don't dig or cut roots of a tree or other wild plant unless you are trying to damage it or it is nursery propagated in volume.

I love fruits in the wild. I couldn't believe that you have fruit like the American pawpaw, with its mango-banana flavors for an exotic sorbet. And of course wild blueberries have much more intense flavor than cultivated types. But in my mind "wild" fruit includes fruit from trees that were originally planted. There are many old farmhouses or semi-urban untended fruit trees such as crabapples, plums, old quince, or mulberries. Although permission must always be obtained from the owner of the land or the tree, many owners or caretakers think these fruits are unsightly, a real nuisance. The fruits may look ugly and ill-formed, but I find them to be beautiful and open to delicious possibilities. And because they are not picked and sorted according to rules, I can get much more variability in type, flavor, and the entire cycle of ripeness.

Unripe Fruits and Nuts

I often think about each stage of a plant. Why is it only good at one time, when we consider it ripe?

Of course we only see the fruit or plant at one stage in the market. Foraging in the field (both farm fields and in the wild) lets us expand the possible flavors and textures of produce beyond that snapshot in time.

I come from a country where the growing season is very short for crops. We are impatient waiting for ripening, so we start looking at things before they are "ripe." It is true, unripe fruits are not as sweet as ripe, but they can have a great acidity that is savory. (I really don't like some of the ripe fruit I find. It is sometimes too sweet or very watery. *Watery* and *juicy* are totally different.)

Pickling can be used to take advantage of the firmness and crispness of fruits that are unripe.

Unripe fruits can be soft with a pleasing crunch. Pick them when the berries are still firm and tart. I like to serve unripe wild wineberries with tartare and wood sorrel or unripe mulberries and green strawberries with homemade cheese and young almonds.

Fruits that are completely hard and green, such as blueberries and wild grapes, are wonderful pickled. Brine first in salt water and then refrigerate or add sharper flavor with vinegar. (See also the Brine-Pickled or Vinegar-Pickled Watermelon Rind recipe on page 141 or the Brined Cucumber recipe on page 120 or the Pickled Green Almonds on page 262.)

Brining fruits is not so farfetched if you think about how much people use and enjoy capers. Capers are the green buds of a Mediterranean shrub. After brining, they are salty and add a salty-pickle spark to many different dishes. For me, a wild bud or underripe fruit that I brine myself is more flavorful and exciting than a store-bought bottled caper. I use wild capered fruits scattered on dishes such as asparagus, purslane, and homemade ricotta cheese.

PICKLED GREEN ALMONDS

Underripe almonds (almonds are actually fruits, not nuts) can also be delicious, with a fresh, green taste that feels younger and lighter. I love green almonds but can find them in the markets for only a short time each year. The first stage of the green almond is when there is no nut inside, just the fuzzy fruit. The inside is gel-like. The second stage (I call it the middle-aged green almond) is when the nut is forming but the outside husk is still soft and has not formed a hard brown shell. Both stages are fine, but once the outside shell is brown and hard, you can't eat that shell. When you pickle them, green almonds taste almost like olives, but with the young nuts on the inside. You can also pickle other unripe nuts, such as unripe green hazelnuts.

You can use pickled green almonds in so many different things. Chop them and make a kind of chutney with lemon and olive oil. Serve with toast or anything that needs some tangy kick. (See for example the photo on page 214.)

4¼ cups water
1 heaping tablespoon kosher salt
¼ pound green almonds or other unripe fruit

Heat the water and salt in a medium pot over medium heat, until the salt is dissolved. Reduce the heat and add the almonds. (I use a Vacupack vacuum sealer in order to keep the green color. If you are just simmering them they may turn dark, but they still taste good.) Simmer for about 20–30 minutes, until soft. The harder the shell is, the longer you have to leave it to become ready. Pour into 2 large mason jars and refrigerate until salty, about 3–4 days.

For serving, remove the almonds from the liquid and slice into ⅛-inch-thick rounds, or about 4 slices per almond.

MAKES ¼ POUND GREEN ALMONDS / TIME: 35 MIN

Flowers

Flowers on cultivated greens often signal to farmers that it is time to throw the plant away because the lettuce or mustard greens have grown old and the plant has "bolted." It is such a waste because these flowers can be delicious and beautiful. Flowers that are not grown purposely for ornamentation (both from vegetables and as true wildflowers) can be more beautiful than a Valentine's Day rose bouquet, having in addition aroma and deliciousness. Some examples are:

CHIVE AND WILD GARLIC FLOWERS: Of the *Allium* genus, both cultivated as well as wild alliums will often produce aerial flowers and bulbets (i.e., bulbs on top the shoot, not underground); both are delicious.

REDBUD FLOWER: The flower of the native redbud tree, *Cercis canadensis*. Indigenous and available as a landscape tree.

ROSE PETALS: *Rosa rugosa,* often found wild at the beach, is Asian in origin. *Rosa virginiana* is less deep in color and a bit more delicate, and indigenous to North America. Wild rose petals are among my favorites. They are a beautiful color and highly fragrant. See the Pickled Wild Rose Petals recipe on page 265.

GREEN CORIANDER FLOWERS AND SEEDS: Coriander leaves are a widely cultivated herb, sold as fresh green leaves. But coriander often *bolts,* meaning it flowers when the days get too warm. This has always been viewed as a sign that the season for farmers is past, and efforts have been made to produce slow-bolting coriander. But the real secret is this: The flowers and green seeds that form after bolting are absolutely delicious and packed with flavor. Use the green seeds in stir-fries, sauces, in both Asian and Western dishes. You can plant coriander in a container on your windowsill or find the seeds and flowers by asking at the farmer's market or visiting an herb farm as the weather starts to turn warm. They may have whole bouquets of the flowers and seeds available. No prep is necessary. Just throw the seeds in stir-fries or sauces. See the Broccoli Stems with Lardo recipe on page 32. You will never buy bottled white coriander seeds again!

MUSTARD FLOWERS: *Brassica* family. People enjoy mustard family plants such as broccoli, bok choy, and cabbage mostly for their greens. However, once the greens mature, they flower and then go to seed. Mustard flowers are fabulous on their own and there are so many different species. The Japanese have a long tradition of pickling and eating mustard flowers as a delicate celebration of the season, not the ending of it.

PICKLED WILD ROSE PETALS

Instead of thinking of flowers only to go with something sweet, think of capturing their fragrance in main dishes, by pickling them. To extend the short season for the petals, I like to pickle them to go with beets, carrots, and fish.

1 cup lightly packed wild rose petals
1 cup apple cider vinegar

Pour the vinegar over the rose petals in a sterilized jar. Cover and refrigerate for up to 6 months.

MAKES ABOUT 1 CUP / TIME: 5 MIN

WEEDS ARE WILD HERBS

I LIKE TO WANDER outdoors in the fields and the orchards, picking the fruits and vegetables. I look at what is planted, at the rows of trees in the orchard or the beets. But I need to see everything that is growing there—both food and weed—without a value judgment. To me, they are the same.

When I go to the sea, it's not just the fish or the oysters, I'm also tasting the briny sea weeds and beach weeds. It's not bad just because it doesn't come in a package with the label "all natural."

There is a word in Danish for weeds, *ukrudt,* which roughly translates as "un-herb." Weeds are considered waste because we have decided they are bad. Just look at all the weed killers and poisons on the market. But whether you call them wild herbs or weeds, they are amazing and delicious.

Seaweeds and Sea Herbs

Seafood almost always means only fish and shellfish, the proteins of the sea. But the sea is a community of edible wildlife, just as meat and plants coexist on the land.

SEAWEEDS

For many people, their sole association with fresh seaweed is walking by (and avoiding) the fishy-smelling slimy brown stuff washed up on beaches. However, seaweed that is stretched, dried, and toasted into sheets—i.e., seaweed as *nori*—is transformed into a great essence of flavor, a bouillon of the sea, loaded with umami.

There is a long history of seaweed use in Nordic countries dating back to at least the tenth century: dulse baked in bread, dried as a snack, used in soups. Asia also has a long history of using seaweed. Professional kitchens regularly use seaweed as an umami flavor enhancement.

Seaweeds are a primary source of omega-3s and have a mineral content that is ten times that of most land plants, and they contain vitamins A, B, C, and E.

I love the weeds of the sea, especially kelp. Sugar kelp I can find off the East Coast of the United States. It is large, brown, and has a great, briny flavor—salty, but deeper, and with some hints of minerals.

The easiest way to enjoy fresh kelp is to dip it briefly in a pot of boiling water. You'll see how the color changes from brown to living green in a few seconds. (Better than a chemistry class!) Remove and slice the warm, green, mild kelp into slivers and use it to top grilled fish drizzled with an herb oil and Parmesan Rind Broth (page 213).

Seaweed can also be dried, aged, and grated like a fine cheese. In Japan, drying seaweed is a labor-intensive, artisanal craft (see page 272 for sources). Konbu (dried kelp) is the foundation for a dashi broth, which I use in Smoky Potato Scrap Broth (page 84) and Sweet & Salty Fish Collars (page 184). Seaweed vinegar powder is on the Puffed Fish Skins (page 188). Other seaweeds that I favor are sea lettuce and dulse. Dulse has long been used in Scandinavia, but I can also get applewood-smoked dulse from Maine.

SEA HERBS

Fresh sea herbs have a mineral-y, briny taste that you can't get from a salt shaker. Small leaves and tips of orache, sea purslane, sea rocket, sea blite, and sea beans grow in coastal areas of North America (as well as on the shores of Denmark). These are some of my favorites; only a small amount adds a big burst of flavor to almost any dish.

A note on sustainability: Beach herbs should be harvested very sparingly and never pulled out due to their important relationship with beach ecology as well as their role preventing dune erosion.

Wild Herbs Glossary

Below are only a few selections out of the abundance of weeds on this earth. Find your own around you, and remember to think twice before you kill them and throw them away.

CHICKWEED: *Stellaria media* is originally from Europe and Asia and is now found throughout North America as a typical garden weed; look for it in between farm rows and other disturbed ground. A small low-sprawling herb, with opposite leaves with pointed tips, chickweed has a mild flavor and can be eaten both cooked and raw.

DANDELION: *Taraxacum officinale* is an herbaceous plant that is one of the most commonly recognized weeds found in Asia, Europe, and North America. Leaves, flowers, and roots are all edible; the leaves contain seven times the amount of phytonutrients as spinach. Younger leaves, before the plant has flowered, are less bitter.

LAMBSQUARTERS: Also known as fat hen and goosefoot, *Chenopodium album* originated in Europe and has now become a common weed in farm fields and gardens and other disturbed ground. It grows upright as an herb with leaves most often shaped like a goose's foot, with a powdery white film that disappears when cooked. A delicious leafy vegetable.

MUSTARDS AND MUSTARD FLOWERS: The young leaves of different *Brassica* species can be peppery when young. The yellow mustard flowers and seeds are juicy, sweet, and have a kick. Both bolted cultivated mustards (such as Asian mizuna, bok choy) as well as wild mustards (dame's rocket or field mustard) have flowers that are sweet and delicious.

PASSIONFLOWERS: A weedy vinelike perennial, *Passiflora incarnata* is also known as maypop in the South. All parts of the plant are edible and make a soothing tea.

PEPPER SMARTWEED: *Polygonum punctatum* is an upright indigenous herb found in moist or wet open sites. The seed is peppery tasting and was used by some Native Americans as seasoning.

PHLOX FLOWERS: Native to the United States, *Phlox paniculata* can be planted as a garden perennial, attracting hummingbirds and pollinators in the summer. The flowers are sweet and bloom through the summer. Please only purchase nursery-propagated stock and do not harvest from the wild, because phlox is a declining native species.

PURSLANE TIPS: *Portulaca oleracea* is a low-growing sprawling weed of disturbed grounds, gardens, and farm fields. The leaves are fleshy and succulent like a cactus, and about ½ inch to 1 inch in size.

SHISO (PERILLA): *Perilla frutescens* is an herb of Asian origin, invasive in gardens and fields in eastern United States and noted for its frilly leaf and aromatic flavor.

SORREL, WILD YELLOW WOODSORREL: This small herb, *Oxalis stricta*, grows to 6 to 8 inches, with three-part leaves that look like a clover but are heart shaped. The plant is indigenous but commonly weedy with a tart, lemony flavor.

Opposite: Field mustard (*brassice rapa*) and redbud flower

AFTERWORD

Agriculture, Waste, and Weeds

Nearly half (45 percent) of the land in the United States is dedicated to agriculture—that is, to producing food. Making food, on an industrial scale, requires significant resources, not only in acres of land, but also millions of gallons of water, plus pesticides, herbicides, fertilizer, and machinery. On a global scale, food productivity (yields per acre) has made measurable gains: Food production increased 150 percent while additional land area only increased 12 percent. However, this rate of productivity is starting to slow: 25 percent of the land on earth that was once productive is now deemed "degraded." Land that is degraded no longer has adequate soil nutrients and water to produce food. Most important: The resources to produce food are not keeping pace with the demand for food. More than ever, wasting 40 percent of food (and everything that is entailed in producing that food) doesn't make common sense.

Of the food that is being produced on available land acreage, the number of plant species is relatively few, lacking in diversity compared to what could be. The Food and Agriculture Organization (FAO) of the United Nations considers diversification of edible food species a high priority for the future security of global food supplies. The FAO has appealed to managers of land in every country to deepen their knowledge and usage of wild edible plants as integral to stewardship and every land management plan.

What are these special wild edible plants? Many of them are underappreciated "weeds." Weeds are the survivors of drought, blight, and pests. Since they have not been domesticated, they have been forced to cope on their own (as plants do in nature), relying on their own chemical and biological defenses. Interestingly, many of these chemical compounds function, when consumed by humans, as phytonutrients and antioxidants. Jo Robinson explains in *Eating on the Wild Side:* "Purslane has six times more vitamin E than spinach and fourteen times more omega-3 fatty acids. It has seven times more beta carotene than carrots." It should be no surprise then that Michael Pollan's *In Defense of Food* names purslane and lambsquarters, common weeds found around the world, as the two most nutritious plants on the planet. Despite herculean efforts and dollars spent to eradicate wild, untamed weeds, these plants still persist, against all odds. Rather than accepting defeat against the wild weedy plants of the earth, it is worth considering how wild plants can have a beneficial place in the future of food on the planet. And maybe, once we invite a few into our kitchen, we might even start to look at the energies we use to eradicate them as the ultimate food waste.

Opposite: Mads Refslund at Comeback Farm among the bounty of pea plants and wild weeds (lambsquarters and amaranth).

RESOURCES

BRANS: Wheat bran and rice brans are available at Bob's Red Mill, bobsredmill.com.

CANNING: For information about canning, see Madelaine Bulwinkel's *Gourmet Preserves Chez Madelaine*. Also, Ball (jars) has step-by-step guides for canning on their website. *More About Canning: Step-by-Step Guides,* www.freshpreserving.com/step-by-step-inside.html.

DEHYDRATORS: Dehydrators are available in multiple sizes and prices at Excalibur (www.excaliburdehydrator.com) and Cabela's (www.cabelas.com).

FOOD WASTE: National Resources Defense Council, "Food Waste," provides information about political and economic issues of food waste and also personal strategies you can adopt to reduce food waste: nrdc.org/issues/food-waste.

> **The Food Waste Challenge** from the USDA offers tools and resources to meet the ambitious goals set to reduce food waste in the United States: usda.gov/oce/foodwaste/.

> **End Food Waste Now** was designed by Diane Hatz to inform consumers and provide tips about what they can do: endfoodwastenow.org.

> **For donating food waste** from your home vegetable garden to food banks, see Gary Oppenheimer's award-winning website: ampleharvest.org.

> To get involved with **Chip Paillex's organization** (page 93), see: www.americasgrowarow.org.

FORAGING AND PLANT IDENTIFICATION: More information at the Plant ID Forum at meadowsandmore.com. For tree identification, see *The Tree Identification Book* by George W. D. Symonds (William Morrow).

GRAINS: Specialty grain products such as broken-rice grits, groats, rye flour, rye berries, as well as rice and wheat brans are available from Anson Mills (ansonmills.com).

PICKLING: In addition to Sandor Katz's *The Art of Fermentation* (see Works Consulted), a favorite starter guide is *Asian Pickles: Sweet, Sour, Salty, Cured and Fermented Preserves from Korea, Japan, China, India and Beyond* by Karen Solomon (Ten Speed Press).

PONZU: Ponzu sauce is available from Eden Foods (edenfoods.com).

PRESERVING AND DRYING: See *Bar Tartine: Techniques & Recipes* by chefs Nicolaus Balla and Cortney Burns (Chronicle Books); also, the National Center for Home Preservation at the University of Georgia: nhcfp.uga.edu

SEAFOOD SUSTAINABILITY: Seafood Watch from the Monterey Bay Aquarium assigns a red, yellow, or green color to seafood to help consumers make sustainable choices in seafood purchases: More info at seafoodwatch.org.

SEAWEEDS, DRIED: Konbu, arame, and others are available from Eden Foods (edenfoods.com).

SPIRALIZER: The Paderno spiralizer (www.padernousa.com/4-blade-spiralizer/) is available online and in stores.

STOVES: Tabletop butane stoves, often used for hotpots, are available from several sources online or at Asian grocery stores.

UMEBOSHI: Sour plum (umeboshi) paste is available from Eden Foods, edenfoods.com.

VINEGAR: Vinegar is a fermented product made from food that contains natural sugars, which ferment into alcohol and then are converted into vinegar. The taste is due to the fermented acetic acid and flavor depends on the base food and time. For more in-depth information, see *The Artisanal Vinegar Maker's Handbook* by Bettina Malle and Helge Schmickl (Spikehorn Press).

THE LARGER
IMPACT

FOOD WASTE is not just about food but also the time, energy, and labor that goes into producing that food. Every piece of food that is thrown away, particularly into the garbage bin, multiplied by each household, has implications beyond wasting that small scrap.

Some facts on the impact of food production on the earth's resources:

WATER: More than 80 percent of water production is used for growing and producing food, and 25 percent of all fresh water in the United States is used for producing food that eventually goes to waste.

LAND: More than half the land in the U.S. is used for food production. In addition, considerable energy and resources are devoted to producing that food and bringing it to the table. Reducing food waste by consumers by 30 percent could save roughly 100 million acres of cropland by 2030.

LANDFILL SATURATION: Uneaten food rotting in landfills is the single largest component of U.S. municipal solid waste. The EPA has catalogued 37 million metric tons of food scraps in 2013, of which only 2 million were composted. The rest went to landfills. Although, ultimately, food scraps are organic and therefore biodegradable, food that makes its way to a landfill remains unchanged after 30 or 40 years and can even still be putrefying after 2,000 years. If food waste were a country, it would be number three in greenhouse gas emissions, right in line behind the United States and China.

Besides, food that is wasted is food that is not going to a hungry mouth. As populations experience more abundance, they adopt more wasteful food consumption habits. Globally, $750 billion worth of food is lost or wasted annually, and yet 870 million people around the world go hungry every day. In the United States, one out of every eight persons is food insecure. It's an important part of the picture for a world with decreasing natural resources and increasing population. In fact, in September 2015, the U.S. Environmental Protection Agency and Department of Agriculture made it an ambitious but essential national goal to reduce food waste by 50 percent by 2030.

WORKS CONSULTED

INTRODUCTION   Redzepi, René. *Rene Redzepi: A Work in Progress.* London: Phaidon, 2013.

CHAPTER 1   Bloom, Jonathan. *American Wasteland: How America Throws Away Nearly Half of Its Food (And What We Can Do About It).* Boston: DaCapo Lifelong Books, 2010.

Gunders, Dana. *Waste-Free Kitchen Handbook: A Guide to Eating Well and Saving Money by Wasting Less Food.* San Francisco: Chronicle, 2015.

Human Microbiome Project. National Institutes of Health. hmpdacc.org/.

Katz, Sandor Ellix. *The Art of Fermentation: An In-Depth Exploration of Essential Concepts and Processes from around the World.* New York: Chelsea Green, 2013.

Leib, E. B. and D. Gunders. "The Dating Game: How Confusing Date Labels Lead to Food Waste in America." Harvard Law School and Natural Resources Defense Council, 2013.

Pollan, Michael. "Some of My Best Friends Are Germs." *The New York Times,* May 15, 2003. www.nytimes.com/2013/05/19/magazine/say-hello-to-the-100-trillion-bacteria-that-make-up-your-microbiome.html. You can participate in the American Gut Project at http://humanfoodproject.com/americangut/.

Rathje, William L., and Cullen Murphy. *Rubbish!: The Archaeology of Garbage.* New York: HarperCollins, 1992.

United Nations Food and Agriculture Organization, et al. *The State of Food Insecurity in the World.* 2012. www.fao.org/docrep/016/i3027e/i3027e.pdf.

United Nations Food and Agriculture Organization. *Global Food Losses and Food Waste—Extent, Causes and Prevention.* 2011. www.fao.org/docrep/014/mb060e/mb060e.pdf.

United States Department of Agriculture Economic Research Service. *The Estimated Amount, Value, and Calories of Postharvest Food Losses at the Retail and Consumer Levels in the United States.* 2014. www.ers.usda.gov/media/1282296/eib121.pdf.

United States Department of Agriculture, Office of the Chief Economist, Food Waste Challenge FAQ. www.usda.gov/oce/foodwaste/faqs.htm.

World Resources Institute. "Reducing Food Loss and Waste," June 2013; see particularly the development of global protocols for measuring food loss and food waste. www.wri.org/sites/default/files/reducing_food_loss_and_waste.pdf.

WRAP (Waste and Resources Action Plan). *The Food We Waste.* 2008. www.ifr.ac.uk/waste/Reports/WRAP%20The%20Food%20We%20Waste.pdf.

CHAPTER 2 Environmental Working Group. "Dirty Dozen: EWG's Shopper's Guide to Pesticides in Produce." www.ewg.org/foodnews/dirty_dozen_list.php.

Patterson, Daniel. "Carrots are the New Caviar" *Financial Times,* June 13, 2009. www.ft.com/cms/s/0/6b9bd7bc-56dd-11de-9a1c-00144feabdc0.

Toussaint-Samat, Maguelonne. *A History of Food.* Hoboken: Wiley-Blackwell, 2009.

CHAPTER 3 Natural Resources Defense Council. *Left Out: An Investigation of Fruit and Vegetable Losses on the Farm.* Issue brief no. 12-12-A, 2012. www.nrdc.org/sites/default/files/crop-shrink-IB.pdf.

CHAPTER 5 Johns Hopkins Center for a Livable Future. "Nearly Half of U.S. Seafood Supply Is Wasted." 2015. http://www.jhsph.edu/news/news-releases/2015/nearly-half-of-u-s-seafood-supply-is-wasted.html.

CHAPTER 8 Bulwinkel, Madelaine. *Gourmet Preserves Chez Madelaine.* Evanston, Ill.: Surrey Books, 2005.

CHAPTER 9 Bloom, Jonathan. *American Wasteland: How America Throws Away Nearly Half of Its Food (and What We Can Do about It).* Boston: Da Capo Lifelong Books, 2010.

Ottolenghi, Yotam. *Plenty More: Vibrant Vegetable Cooking from London's Ottolenghi.* Emeryville, Calif.: Ten Speed Press, 2014.

United States Department of Agriculture, "Leftovers and Food Safety." June 15, 2013. www.fsis.usda.gov/wps/portal/fsis/topics/food-safety-education/get-answers/food-safety-fact-sheets/safe-food-handling/leftovers-and-food-safety/ct_index.

CHAPTER 10 Mouritsen, Ole G., Jonas Drotner Mouritsen, and Mariela Johansen. *Seaweeds: Edible, Available, and Sustainable.* Chicago: University of Chicago Press, 2013.

AFTERWORD Food and Agriculture Organization of the United Nations. "The State of the World's Land and Water Resources for Food and Agriculture—Managing Systems at Risk." 2011. www.fao.org/docrep/017/i1688e/i1688e.pdf.

Pollan, Michael. *In Defense of Food: An Eater's Manifesto.* New York: Penguin, 2008.

Robinson, Jo. *Eating on the Wild Side: The Missing Link to Optimum Health.* New York: Little, Brown, 2013.

ACKNOWLEDGMENTS

Thanks from Mads to my mom, **YVONNE LYKKE HURUM**, for framing my first pizza and hanging it on the wall to give me support in my first childhood cooking endeavor, and to my dad, **CARSTEN REFSLUND**, for your support and guidance; and to **MY SISTERS** for serving as such agreeable guinea pigs for my cook-ing experiments. And of course…a special thank-you from Mads to **KELLY** for your unwavering support.

The idea for this book was stop and go for a while but here we are, happy, and with grateful thanks to all the incredibly talented people who were instrumental in getting us to this point. Thanks to photographers **ANDREA, MARTY, MOE** for your inspiration of the beauty in trash, for endless days and nights on "the porch," for ceramic colors of the sky and sea, and for going above and beyond.

To **SHAUN WIDGER** for your commitment to deliciousness, global culinary experience, and precise methodology; we will always remember the pumpkin marathon day and rambling through the orchard stuffing fallen fruits in your pockets.

To **RYAN KEELAN** for your enthusiasm, hard work, culinary innovation, and a mind like a steel trap for exact measurements. Forever grateful for insightful texted solutions at all hours of the day and night. Book event in Charleston?

To **JOSEPH YARDLEY** for your patience and good humor (within limits) going along with Mads's brainstorm of an idea to turn a bucket of pig's blood over your head and for your passion for the "project" that never began…

To **SARAH VILLAMERE** for your extra hard work, talent, and experience in translating wasted and wild ingredient dishes to exact-measurement recipes, to your professional sense of proportions, and to being able to help translate a muttered "nine grams" into something amazing.

To **MICHAEL REYNOLDS** for lovely cocktail creations and the requisite group tastings and toastings at your bar, Black Crescent.

To **ASHLEY BARE**, thanks for your game sense of adventure, and especially for lending your experience in teaching all those pasta and cooking classes to test and make things work.

To **JADE GREENE**, for trying out admittedly unusual recipes at home and your pleasant surprise when they tasted delicious, and for your invaluable reflective tester's notes.

To **MAYFIELD WILLIAMS**, for your patience and perseverance in testing these recipes on your loved ones.

Thank you to **COMEBACK FARMS**, **MOUNTAIN MEADOW FARMS**, and **GROW A ROW FARMS** for their generosity and letting us ramble and partake of the bounty of their lands.

To **MARK DRABICH**, experienced and ebullient fishmonger, for handing over odd bits of fish and scales at the fish market counter while wowing the gathering crowd, and thank you for your tips on storage and prep.

To **LENA STRUWE**, botanical director of the Chrysler Herbarium and curator of the blog botanicalaccuracy.com, for your humorous advice on the naming of parts of plants.

And for the sound and soothing counsel of our agent, **SHARON BOWERS**, and our wonderful and ever optimistic editors, **KAREN MURGOLO**, **BECKY MAINES**, and **MORGAN HEDDEN**, and designer **LAURA PALESE**, thank you for believing in the delicious possibilities of cooking with wasted food.

Finally in special gratitude to **KELLY ELIVO**, and to **WIL**, **REBECCA**, **GEORGIA**, and **MIA WONG** for their support and patient tolerance in finding strange things bubbling, dehydrating, and fermenting in corners of our abodes, never knowing when it was finally okay to throw something out.

INDEX

ABOUT THE AUTHORS

Mads Refslund was born in Denmark, attended culinary school, and is one of the co-founders of Noma, which has repeatedly been named the greatest restaurant in the world. Mads left to run his own Michelin-starred restaurant in Denmark, MR, then moved to New York City, where he created the menu at ACME NYC. *The New York Times* awarded it two stars for successfully integrating Nordic philosophy with North American seasonal ingredients. He is opening a new seasonal restaurant in New York.

Tama Matsuoka Wong is a renowned forager for chefs such as Daniel Boulud, Marc Forgione, Claus Meyer, and others. She is also the author of *Foraged Flavor*. Her website is MeadowsandMore.com.